"The 5% Rule of Leadership *is an original blueprint we all need to study for the challenges ahead: organizations can truly blossom only when technological innovation and growth ambitions are tamed by a strong sense of purpose, an inspirational mission statement, and a fundamental reprioritization of any company's most valuable asset: their employees.*"

—Marlene Pelage
global chief finance officer of Gen II Fund Services LLC
NetScout board member

"Anil Singhal addresses some important engagement lessons in this book starting with humanity and trust, but the one that struck me the most was that the 5% Rule saves time and money. It spares your talented team from wasting their time, and it insulates everybody from the nightmare of getting involved in a failed project that has too much momentum to redirect or stop. It forces you to establish the way in which you want events to unfold. It forces you to take charge of your destiny. From experience, this is true: the 5% Rule can work as an operating philosophy for the entire company affecting both profitability and efficiency for any organization. As a leader, if you take command of the situation at the start, it becomes your choice what trajectory you want the story to take. The 5% Rule is gold. However, dig deeper—there are so many other refreshing nuggets and perspectives in this must-read book—especially on the entrepreneur journey."

—Andrew J. Nash
founder and managing partner
UpOver Ventures

"Anil's philosophy and leadership perspective are inspiring, enduring, and relevant for businesspeople and leaders seeking a unique and compelling new way of running a company that can last for

generations. His 5% Rule and approach to developing a vibrant corporate culture have helped him create a company that prides itself in being Guardians of the Connected World."

—Tiffani Bova
executive advisor
and author of the best-selling books
The Experience Mindset and *Growth IQ*

"Anil Singhal brilliantly explores the merits of the 5% Rule, analogous to the Pareto principle, to showcase that, in an era of ruthless efficiency for the sake of short-term profits, there is another way of leading teams and businesses successfully. Drawing from a multitude of personal experiences and anecdotes at NetScout, Anil, with deep humility, pragmatic simplicity, but undeniable conviction, shares with the reader invaluable pearls of wisdom to hone on their leadership skills and sharpen their business acumen. This truly inspirational book shatters traditional management principles and instead advocates for a leadership style and business approach that are rooted in humanity, respect, empowerment, and loyalty. The 5% Rule of Leadership is an original blueprint we all need to study for the challenges ahead: organizations can truly blossom only when technological innovation and growth ambitions are tamed by a strong sense of purpose, an inspirational mission statement, and a fundamental reprioritization of any company's most valuable asset: their employees. A book you must read: compelling, beautifully written, and tightly argued, it offers a refreshing viewpoint on leading organizations with deep humanity and clarifying focus."

—Marlene Pelage
global chief finance officer of Gen II Fund Services LLC
NetScout board member

"As I delved into Anil's work, a mirrored reflection of my own journey unfolded before me. Despite my enterprise being significantly smaller than Anil's, I found a deep resonance with his ideas and, more profoundly, with the values he champions within his business. Equity, transparency, empathy, and the centrality of the human element are not universally

embraced at the executive level; yet, when applied with deliberate intention, they foster tangible successes for individuals and, consequently, for the entire organization. After all, a company without its human core is nothing.

Anil's book stands out not just as an engaging read but also as a beacon that leaves a lasting imprint on the reader, inspiring leaders at every level to cultivate a workplace where human values are not just adjuncts but also the cornerstone of business success. It is a powerful affirmation that inclusive and ethical leadership practices can be successfully implemented in business environments of every scale.

This testament by Anil is not merely a call for reflection but a clarion call to action for those prepared to listen and embrace a way of leading and conducting business that places people at its heart. In my opinion, his book is an essential read for anyone aspiring to transform their work environment and the broader business landscape into a place of greater justice, transparency, and empathy where every individual can find fulfillment and satisfaction."

—Antonio Grasso
Digital Business Innovation Srl

"Anil Singhal's book is a must-read for anyone wanting to be a successful entrepreneur and build a sustainable company. His success has resulted primarily from this key principle: a 'not mean' humanistic culture centered on employee-first values, fairness, and purpose, which results in high employee engagement, which results in satisfied customers, which results in continual business success!"

—Edward D. Hess
professor emeritus
Darden Business School
University of Virginia
and the author of *OWN YOUR WORK JOURNEY!*
*The Path to Meaningful Work and Happiness
in the Age of Smart Technology and Radical Change*

THE 5%

RULE OF
LEADERSHIP

THE
5%
RULE OF
LEADERSHIP

USING LEAN DECISION-MAKING TO DRIVE TRUST, OWNERSHIP, AND TEAM PRODUCTIVITY

ANIL K. SINGHAL

WILEY

Published by John Wiley & Sons, Inc., Hoboken, New Jersey.
Published simultaneously in Canada.

For general information on our other products and services or for technical support, please contact our Customer Care Department within the United States at (800) 762-2974, outside the United States at (317) 572-3993 or fax (317) 572-4002.

Wiley also publishes its books in a variety of electronic formats. Some content that appears in print may not be available in electronic formats. For more information about Wiley products, visit our web site at www.wiley.com.

Library of Congress Cataloging-in-Publication Data is Available:

ISBN 9781394285136 (cloth)
ISBN 9781394285150 (epub)
ISBN 9781394285143 (epdf)

Cover Design & Image: Wiley
Author Photo: Courtesy of the Author

SKY10080519_080124

This book is dedicated to my family for their unquestioned support, and to my friends at NETSCOUT, who I have had the privilege of working with and learning from. You all have helped me shape the values, philosophy, and techniques described in this book over the last 30 years.

Contents

Acknowledgments

I would like to thank Steve Morgan for the book cover design and Azar Khansari and Donna Candelori for the meticulous edits of the manuscript.

Foreword

You may not recognize the name Anil Singhal, but I guarantee that by the time you finish this book, you will know it well. That is because Anil has been Silicon Valley's leading iconoclast—and I mean that in the best way possible. He also is likely one of the most innovative leaders that the tech industry has seen in a half-century.

Anil is the cofounder, president, and CEO of NetScout, a leading maker of products that help customers monitor the reliability and security of their business networks. NetScout's motto captures well the company's role in the internet universe: "The Guardians of the Connected World."

Over the last 30-plus years, Anil and his team have built NetScout from nothing to a very successful company approaching $1 billion in annual revenues. It has done so in good times and bad, with some of the highest levels of employee retention and morale and customer loyalty.

It is precisely NetScout's low profile that has enabled Anil to conduct his ongoing experiment in building a successful, enduring, and most of all fair company. It has enabled him to work in relative isolation. He hasn't drunk Silicon Valley Kool-Aid or made his moves in the media limelight. Instead, he has spent the last three decades continuously trying one radical initiative after another to build a great company designed to last generations. In an industry where company lifespans are measured in months, and the most common business strategy is to cash out by being acquired, NetScout has refused multiple merger entreaties—and plans to be around for the long haul. It has succeeded because Anil has turned NetScout into a laboratory of management science, questioning business aphorisms, experimenting with new techniques, throwing out what doesn't work, and adopting what does. He is a true pragmatist: his only criteria have been to do what works—all under the constraint of treating his employees, investors, and customers honestly.

It hasn't been easy. As Anil admits in the pages that follow, he has followed blind alleys and made his share of mistakes. But he has never given up his vision of a great company.

He began with one department, then another. In time, nearly the entire company was operating in a new and revolutionary way. Employees have stayed, sales have grown, and NetScout's products have become an industry standard. That vision is of a company that is Lean in its operations, while at the same time Not Mean.

Most business schools (and CEOs) will tell you that this goal is unachievable, that such a circle cannot be squared. But Anil will tell you that a Lean But Not Mean company is possible. That what seems like radical new processes and operations soon becomes not only reasonable, but logical—and most of all successful. It is possible to build a great company without sacrificing its soul.

But it is the vehicle for building a Lean But Not Mean company that is Anil's most important innovation: he calls it the *5% Rule*.

The 5% Rule is the most trust-based management technique imaginable. Anil devised it in response to two phenomena that kept reappearing in the company's operation. The first he observed during negotiations. Whether with vendors or when the company was acquiring another company, Anil discovered to his dismay there was a tendency for these negotiations to morph as they proceeded. Terms were changed, price suddenly became a matter of dispute, and the process inevitably dragged on far longer than needed.

The second phenomenon he observed occurred whenever the company embarked on a new initiative. Inevitably, the effort would begin to go sideways as the company got distracted by another new opportunity or management diverted the program to pursue one of their own pet ideas. The result was always more delayed, costly, and far less competitive than the original plan.

Even worse, Anil came to realize, was that this was accepted as standard procedure—a normal cost of doing business—in most of the industrial world. Anil, as is his way, refused to accept the status quo. Instead, he moved all key decision-making—including the price of a business deal—to the start of the process. As a leader, this is where he, too, devotes most of his attention.

Then, once these decisions were made, unless some extraordinary event occurred, they were all but inviolate. Anil handed them off to the managing team and went back to his other duties. If the company to be acquired balked at the acquisition price, NetScout walked away. If a different business opportunity suddenly appeared, NetScout did not pursue it. And Anil returned to the initiative only when it was approaching completion, to close out the paperwork and to celebrate their success with the team.

In time, this concept of front-loading all the tough decisions at the beginning led to Anil nicknaming this technique the 5% Rule, as that figure represented the time he devoted on any project.

Then, as the years passed it became apparent to Anil that what he had developed in piecemeal was, in fact, an encompassing vision of how to run any organization properly if it were to realize his vision of Lean But Not Mean. It was the best and most novel way to run Lean operations. But, even more important, as the years passed, Anil ultimately came to realize that his 5% Rule was the best leadership technique for every department of NetScout—and not just at the top, but at all levels throughout the company.

The 5% Rule guaranteed that every action the company took would be well thought out at the beginning, and not just driven by speculation or excitement. It was the ultimate "fail-fast" strategy.

Further, those actions would remain disciplined through completion because willy-nilly deviation was not possible. Finally, the 5% Rule reinforced consistency in purpose and adherence to the fundamental rules of fairness and honesty that were at the heart of NetScout's core values.

It has taken Anil decades, but in the last few years his 5% Rule and Lean But Not Mean philosophy have come together in a vision of how to build a great, enduring, and admirable enterprise. And that is why now he is emerging into the public eye to share his stunning vision with the business world.

How did Anil Singhal, of all people, devise this theory? I have a hypothesis about that.

Anil is a classic outsider. Born in India, he has lived in America now for more than 40 years—a highly successful citizen of his adopted country, yet still with strong ties to his homeland. He runs a company headquartered in a quiet suburb closer to the New Hampshire border than to the tech hub of Boston, and far removed from the Silicon Valley heart of the digital world, and yet successfully competes with most of the behemoths of his industry.

Together, these factors—combined with his naturally independent, even nonconformist personality—have freed Anil to approach the challenge of running a company in an oblique and unique way. In other words, the very reason you have not heard of him is one of the reasons he could devise his Lean But Not Mean philosophy and the powerful tool of the 5% Rule. Or it's just because Anil sees the world in a different, orthogonal way—and has found that it works.

For now, the important thing to appreciate is that the approach presented by this book challenges the conventional notions of how to start and grow a great company. And the more you study its message, the more logical, humane, and practical it becomes.

Many of the ideas presented in the pages that follow may seem counterintuitive, even illogical. But give Anil a chance. His explanations will surprise you. Apply them in your business, and they will enlighten you. Adopt them into your corporate culture, and it may change you and your company forever.

Anil Singhal is an important, radical thinker. His ideas deserve to be heard, and, if you are intrigued enough, to be applied.

Michael S. Malone

Sunnyvale, California

Introduction

I n an era of perpetual and rapid change, this book argues for deliberation.

At a time when the accepted business philosophy is to get under way as soon as possible and make course corrections on the fly, this book offers a strategy for making your key decisions up front.

In an era of regular layoffs during downturns. Of rewarding company superstars more highly than the rank-and-file. Of creating different classes of stock for different management levels. And of jettisoning veteran employees after they have been with the firm for more than a few years. This book counsel's fairness, and equivalent treatment, and aspiring to keep your employees not just until they retire, but even after. It's what I have come to call a *Not Mean* culture—a culture that centers on people-first values, fairness, and purpose.

When we founded NetScout, my motive from the beginning was not benevolence or an overdeveloped sense of fairness. It was based on pragmatism—that is, what worked. But, in time, I came to realize through trial and error, that fairness needed to be the heart of the company. Why? Fairness drives transparency, which in turn enables simplicity. These factors have proven to be a great foundation for what I refer to as *Lean* decision-making—a set of techniques that I have developed over time to help me navigate the myriad choices any leader confronts on a regular basis.

Happily, being in a niche business—corporate information infrastructure—I was able to observe and interact with the many famous, and soon-to-be famous, technology companies without risk of takeover or competitive intervention. I saw how many of those companies laid off employees on a regular basis. How they sometimes drove out anyone with too much tenure under the misconceived premise that they could no longer be innovative contributors. And I read how the executives of many of those companies got extraordinarily rich while leaving their hard-working employees unrewarded. Both my wife and I had experienced inexplicable and seemingly capricious layoffs in the early part of our professional careers—and we did not want to inflict that type of unsettling cruelty on others.

Much of this shocked me; but what really appalled me was how many of the employees of these companies suffered from low morale and were ready to find new jobs whenever they got the chance. I knew the lore of Silicon Valley, and that founding Valley companies had not always been this way. Something had changed in their values and everyday workers were bearing the brunt of that change.

I resolved to find another way. The behavior of my neighbors may have been an impetus, but they were not the only reason. I have always been a bit contrary as a leader. I have a natural affinity for simplicity and economy over complexity and expense, for well-considered up-front decisions over rushing headlong into costly and risky new ventures. And I have never believed that treating employees unfairly is anything but a recipe for long-term disaster.

In founding NetScout, my cofounder and I never wanted a quick turnaround, becoming a "pump and dump" company that captured enough market attention to lure a buyer, make the founders rich, and then disappear. Rather, we had wanted the traditional dream of building a great company that lasted generations, produced high-quality products that attracted deep loyalty from customers, and gave its employees the kind of secure employment that enabled them to start families and enjoy stable lives.

You can understand now why my theories of management have sometimes been called "contrary," "anachronistic," and "counterintuitive." And I do not mind, because as I have watched companies come and go over the last three decades, I have become only more convinced that I am right.

NetScout is always aspiring to reach greater and greater heights, not just in terms of attaining profit but also in terms of continuing to meet the needs of our rapidly evolving industry and our global workforce. In the process, we have acquired more than 10 companies, both large and small and including some of Silicon Valley's industry darlings, and navigated the company successfully through profound technological change. Despite economic booms and bust cycles, we have held steady, with an average employee tenure of over 10 years, an average leadership tenure of over 20 years, and the vast majority of talent from acquisitions staying with the company and taking on leadership roles. In other words, we are not an anachronism, but an anomaly—and we think, most of all, that we can be a model of how to build a successful and enduring company that is also fair and transparent to all its stakeholders, most of all, its employees.

The Human Ratio

The 5% Rule can be seen as the embodiment in decision-making of the sociological/statistical theory known as the Pareto principle, devised by Italian mathematician Vilfredo Pareto, and popularized in 1941 by the noted management consultant Joseph Juran.

You know it as the *80/20 rule*, which effectively captures a characteristic of human nature that 20% of people in any field seem to do 80% of the work, and the remaining 80% do just 20% of the work. In the years since, the Pareto principle has been shown to operate in many corners of human existence and in the natural world.

Here is another definition, from Google:

> *The 80/20 rule states that 80% of outcomes are determined by 20% of input. For example, if your goal is to acquire 100 new leads, 80 leads would come from only 20% of what you did to get them. This is why it is important to know how and where your effort makes the most impact—in other words, 20% of the decisions can have 80% of the consequences.*

It is my belief the 80/20 rule applies again to the 20% ("Pareto of Pareto") when it comes to decision-making. That is, I have found that a fraction of decisions result in a majority of consequences.

I had coined this phenomenon the 5% Rule of leadership long before I came to know of the Pareto principle, but I was struck by how congruent they are. The 5% Rule, when applied by the right set of leaders, at the very beginning of an important project, can deliver the Pareto of Pareto promise. To put it another way, 4% of effort (20% of 20%, rounded to my 5%), will invariably deliver 95% of the results all the time for any important project in any and all departments and disciplines of an organization.

It becomes even more interesting when you take the 5% Rule and embed it into the overall operation of an enterprise—that is, the formalization of a 5% solution to management and its formulation of a strategy and plan of execution.

What does all this mean? Nothing—other than it gives valuation to the 5% Rule as being a natural, human model for business decision-making wherever you can apply it.

Moreover, it suggests that you as a leader are justified in devoting your time to any major company action or decision during the earliest phase of that process. It also argues against the traditional notion that the leader's time should be engaged after most of the work has been done, and the team now needs the leader to make a go, no-go decision. Both the 5% Rule and the Pareto Principle argue that this method is inefficient, resulting in wasted efforts, and worse, it can create a momentum that can lead to poor outcomes.

Rather, the 5% Rule argues that the leader's role is to—at the start—determine the real goals of any company initiative, establish the parameters of the project to come, and then decide whether to go ahead or not. In this way, needless expense and effort can be averted, and company resources and talent can be properly devoted—and not wasted on a future dead end.

Learn as You Go

In drafting this book, I have continued to hone my use of the 5% Rule. It has proven more supple, universal, and powerful than we ever would have imagined in NetScout's early days. And I am convinced that it is a lynchpin to successful leadership. And yet, successful leadership cannot take place in a vacuum. It is important to note that although the core values of a company create the Not Mean culture, and the 5% Rule allows Lean decision-making, it is their combination—that is the consistent application of the 5% Rule inside a Not Mean culture—that produces true success. This flies in the face of the old saying that "nice guys finish last." In fact, throughout the course of NetScout history, I have observed the exact opposite to be true: *Nice people finish first*. My goal in this book is not to criticize the practices of other companies that operate differently than NetScout. Instead, my goal is to highlight how this different operating philosophy worked at NetScout, and how it might also work for you. To paraphrase one of my business colleagues, "I am surprised that NetScout has been so successful, despite not being Mean." My answer, "NetScout, in fact, has been successful because of not being Mean, which is largely made possible because of the implementation of the 5% Rule."

In the pages that follow, I look at the many ways that the 5% Rule can be applied to business units and businesses in general. In practice I think you will discover added nuances to make it even more powerful. My hope is that you will pass it on as you journey through your career. I believe that, together, we can spark a quiet and enlightened revolution in the business world . . . and in the process, we can find even greater success on the road to becoming Lean But Not Mean enterprises.

Like any book, this one can be read in the order of its chapters. But I have also organized those chapters into sections reflecting the life cycle of a company— from a start-up to a mature business. Finally, as each chapter functions as a stand-alone narrative, you may also choose to read just the chapters that address a challenge you are facing at this moment—including, ultimately, in the question of succession.

But however you choose to read this book, I hope you will remember that my only goal has been to fill the world with more efficient, more successful, and fairer enterprises—great companies that employees will look back on with pride and affection.

I

Forming a
Great Company
Creating a Strong Foundation

ounding a company is the most chaotic business experience imaginable. A start-up, woefully under-staffed for the task, must develop and prototype the company's first product, tackle all of the bureaucratic tasks of incorporating the business, lease office space and equipment, prepare a viable business plan, recruit top talent, hire contractors, establish supply and retail chains, create a marketing plan, and, not least, go out and raise investment money. If any of these efforts fail, the company is probably doomed.

Understandably, in the face of all these challenges, there is not much attention being paid to what the company values are, what culture it seeks, what purpose it embodies. When you are worried about meeting next week's payroll or searching for that fatal bug in your new product, there is not any time for musing about your company's culture or long-term goals.

And yet, this is precisely the time when you should be thinking about these larger issues. Your new company not only needs to be built but also it needs to be formed. Too many start-up companies are so distracted by their daily crises that they allow their young company to drift into establishing a default culture that is the product of expediency and the unthinking adoption of bad past practices of a previous employer. Then, once the new start-up is under way, it is trapped in improvised rules and patterns from which it is unlikely to ever escape.

Companies can survive weak early products if they have in place a culture that supports innovation and risk. They can survive bad executive decisions if they have an environment that fosters trust and transparency. They can even survive serious market or economic downturns if they have been prudent with money and enjoy loyal employees willing to sacrifice for the company. But, overall, they cannot survive a poisonous and alienating corporate culture. We see examples of that in the business world every day: great companies that eventually stumble and die from their own internal contradictions and bad faith.

This is the reason you need to implant and enforce a worthy corporate culture from the very beginning. It is not just that it will help you succeed, but because the type of success derived from a worthy culture is precisely what will help your company grow in a smart and sustainable way. A company enjoying steady growth—adding new employees, new levels of management, new facilities, and new product lines, all while expanding globally—becomes increasingly difficult to lead. A leader can try to dictate rules of behavior and responsible action, but that employee who is six levels down the organization chart and based half a world away is unlikely to ever get the message. Or worse, they get a garbled, even contradictory message, which is the result of playing a game of telephone tag through a half-dozen intermediaries adding their own spin or misinterpretation of the meaning of the message.

That is why a company's culture—its personality, style, ethics, and rules of behavior—is so much more powerful than anything managed by executive diktat. As a leader, you set the example. By operating the company through people-first and values-centric principles from the very start, you can help cultivate a Not Mean culture. This is the type of strong foundation needed to build a lasting company. The next step is to adopt a decision-making scheme that is flexible enough to apply to any situation, and at the same time rigid enough to ensure consistency. This is where Lean decision-making, and its anchor, the 5% Rule, comes into play.

At its core, the 5% Rule trusts each employee to find the right path toward a goal that you define from the start with the least amount of interference along the way. I think of the 5% Rule (which can only exist within a culture of trust) as establishing the guardrails through which the company's efforts will be channeled, and Lean decision-making as the process by which long-term direction and the end goal are defined. The combination of the 5% Rule, Lean decision-making, and a Not Mean culture results in a uniquely efficient and psychologically safe organization. And it is with this recipe, of employees feeling free to make their own decisions all while operating within a set of principles defined at the beginning, that the fruits of success bloom.

In this section, I suggest some key choices that new companies can make to shape the type of enterprise they want to be. The good news is that these choices can be put into place on day one—and if regularly reinforced, can define your company for decades, even centuries. Moreover, most actually are more efficient and less expensive than their conventional alternatives and provide a much better quality of life to their employees, which may give you more time and money to deal with all the other challenges of starting a company.

1

Deciding First What Is Important
The 5% Rule in Business and Life

It was just a few years after I was hired for my first job in the corporate world as a software engineer that I heard the very American phrase, "Lean and Mean," during one of my employer's internal group meetings. The phrase sounded interesting, even intriguing, at first—something you would want successful leaders and managers to emulate.

It took another couple of years for me to understand the cultural philosophy behind this phrase, as I saw Lean and Mean put into action in many companies, including the one I worked for.

Running a Lean operation, I was told, was important for business survival and success, and so one should be prepared to be Mean to your employees and other stakeholders to meet that corporate goal.

But what I saw in the real world was sudden project cancellations, frequent reorganizations, cost cuttings, and painful layoffs. It all seemed so unnecessary and painful. It not only seemed cruel, but worse: Such a philosophy—even if it worked for a while—never seemed to achieve its long-term goals.

That is why, in September 1984, when I started NetScout with my cofounder, we vowed to run our company differently. Over time, I came to realize that if you could apply Lean decision-making as part of your company's core principles, you might never have to engage in Mean practices. This had an interesting corollary: People and companies who are perceived as Mean may be using this philosophy to cover their less-than-efficient practices—that is, they might be merely "Mean But Not Lean." The *5% Rule of Leadership* was the name we gave to the practice we conceived to implement Lean decision-making. Let me explain.

By the new century, I had now understood that my notion of Lean But Not Mean was describing a destination, an attitude that described the place I wanted my company to reach, and then exemplify. But what was the process for getting there; what were the operational tools I needed for the journey?

It took me another decade to realize that the processes I was using for decision-making in every part of the company—from hiring to manufacturing to acquisition—all had one crucial factor in common: I made all my key decisions at the very start.

Indeed, I noticed all my key decisions were made during the first 5% of the initiative's overall timeline. After that, I inevitably turned it over to the broader NetScout team to work out the details. Only then, at the very end of the process, did I return to close the deal and join the celebration.

It was not lost on me that this was not how most of my peers in tech—frankly, in most of the corporate world—worked. The usual approach was for a CEO to be brought in after the process was under way, fine-tune it, sign off on the plan, and then revisit the program at various intervals all the way through.

Sometimes, this meant that the CEO, well into the project, would change their mind and either kill the initiative or send it off in a different direction. This was true for the rest of the senior leadership, as well.

This struck me as incredibly wasteful of both financial and human capital. Think of the enormous sums that are lost forever when a project that is nearly finished suddenly gets cancelled. Worse, think of the demoralizing effect on loyal employees who have given heart and soul to the project, only to see it peremptorily shut down and themselves laid off.

Instead, why not do all your due diligence up front? In other words, why not decide on the steps before executing on the very first step. Then, armed with sufficient data, make your strategic decisions—and leave it to your smart and loyal employees to work out the tactics? It is so much more economical. It keeps you from interfering with the work (and trust) of your people. And it gives you a metric by which the company can make all its decisions.

The more I looked at this process—which I now called NetScout's *5% Rule*—the more I realized that it was applicable in every part of the company and in everything we did.

If it is useful, think of how you regularly, and unknowingly, apply the 5% Rule to your personal life. When you know you need to go somewhere, you research all the diverse ways in which you can get to your destination: Will I take a car, hail a ride share or taxi, take a train? Without even thinking about it, you are approaching your transportation options as a problem-solver. You reach consensus in your mind or with your fellow travelers on the mode of travel, and then you move into execution mode. That critical first step of thinking through different transportation modes before going into action is the 5% Rule.

Behind Every Decision

There is one very important factor that must be taken into consideration when talking about the 5% Rule, and that is its interconnectivity with your values. For many start-ups, the initial focus might be to go public or to reach certain milestone revenue targets. NetScout in its infancy had a similar focus, and yet those milestones were always secondary to our underlying belief—our underlying value—that success does not come in the form of a number, but rather in the form of a company that holds on to its employees and customers not just for years but for generations. The value we put into our people and our customers is the core of what I call our *Not Mean* culture. That is why, even though we are occasionally approached about being acquired, we always turn away those entreaties. It is why we welcome back ex-employees and have only one class of stock—and most of all, why we struggle so hard to keep all our people.

Even in a place like Silicon Valley, where the typical résumé shows no job lasting more than a couple of years, our people often stay until the day they retire. A company is more than a profit machine: it is a huge part of our lives. We want to look back on our careers as having been part of a family working on worthy things in a common cause.

If I had to distill NetScout's value system into one word, it would be fairness.

It turns out in business that one of the hardest things to do is not beat competition or increase stock value but treat all your employees fairly. To deal with them honestly and transparently. That is because, in practice, it means treating everyone the same way, without fear or favor: the same salary for the same job no matter the tenure, the same percentage bonus, the same stock class, the same vacation time, and the same incentives for everyone.

Do you treat your employees with the same fairness? Could you? Trust me, it is a perpetual challenge. It goes against human nature. But it is a wonderful discipline for management—and it makes leadership so much simpler and transparent.

The consequences of following the 5% Rule reinforce both Lean decision-making and a Not Mean culture: Lean, because it prevents expensive tangents and dead ends; all key choices are made at the very start when no commitments of money, time, or people have been made. And Not Mean because when everyone knows the plan and goal up-front, no one is surprised or can demand special deviation down the line.

The Ultimate Test

The first real test of our Not Mean culture and how far we had come in using the 5% Rule to drive Lean decision-making came during that crazy interval in the late 1990s between the inflation of dot-com hype to the collapse of the dot-com bubble. During that boom we saw some of the highest employee turnover rates in the company's history, but for those who stayed with the company we also built deep loyalties. This gave us an opportunity to fine-tune our operating philosophy and make some practical adjustments. We learned from our mistakes, and we came out with some key conclusions:

- Employees are a company's intellectual property, and they can be a significant competitive advantage.

- The definition of "talent" is not simply good or smart people, but good and smart people who believe in the mission and values of a company.

- You need to treat employees with respect and dignity, even during involuntary terminations, regardless of whose fault it is.

- You need to respect the wishes of employees who may want to leave for greener pastures and be ready to take back some who left for the right reasons, if they do decide to return.

- Everyone makes mistakes sometimes, and in most cases, people deserve a second chance. At the same time, if you let some employees take advantage of your Not Mean value system, then you are not being fair to others who honestly believe in and support that value system.

- As a company, public or private, you have a responsibility to your investors and other stakeholders. So, although it may be admirable to make a Not Mean pledge, such as making sudden cost cuts only as a last resort to keep that pledge, you need to have long-since-implemented Lean decision-making processes.

- Finally, we learned that the 5% Rule still worked in times of both explosive change-driven growth and industry-wide crash. During the former, it stabilized the company and kept it from blindly chasing the next big thing, and during the latter it kept us focused on our core business and keeping our costs at a minimum. We came out of both challenges alive, with our full staff, our customers, and a running start over our competitors in the new 21st century economy.

I am especially proud that the foundation we built then has lived on and continues to deliver great outcomes even today.

Over the last 20 years NetScout has become an industry leader in its key market segments, gaining substantial market share, growing from $100 million to nearly $1 billion in annual revenues. Similarly, NetScout's valuation has increased tenfold during this time. We now have more than 2,000 customers spread over 100 countries, and we employ more than 2,000 people across five continents. Until you opened the pages of this book, you may have never heard of us or what we do. But I assure you that our customers and competitors know who we are. And if your company's information infrastructure has not crashed lately, you can thank us.

Since 2015, after another transformative acquisition (this time, a company one and half times our size), I have started talking more openly about the 5% Rule, Lean decision-making, and our Not Mean culture, all of which have had tremendous impact on NetScout's success, employee morale, talent retention, and innovation. My counterparts in other companies sometimes dismiss this unorthodox philosophy of business as, at best, impractical, and at worst, impossible, even dangerous.

But many of our long-term employees and managers, who have personally experienced the 5% Rule, continued to urge me to promote these ideas beyond NetScout. One employee even told me that after two decades of the usual two-year cycle of hiring and layoff, NetScout was the first job that enabled him to sleep at night and not worry about losing his latest job. I hope everybody at the company feels the same way.

The 5% Rule has now become such an integral part of NetScout's culture that we no longer really think about it. It has become the foundation of our corporate culture. Yet, I have come to realize that preserving the consistent application of the 5% Rule requires ongoing and deliberate effort. Like culture itself, the 5% Rule is only as effective as the people using it.

2

Excited Employees to Satisfied Customers to Happy Shareholders
The Virtuous Spiral

This chapter's title may seem obvious. What company does not want excited, satisfied, and happy employees, customers, and shareholders? But the real, and potentially controversial, secret in this title is that those words are listed in order of priority.

Most enterprises—and many contemporary business theorists—would disagree vehemently with that orientation. The pressure on public companies to maximize shareholder value continues to rise, along with increased regulation, more passive investing options, and activist campaigns. It is my belief that, although management and the board must uphold their fiduciary responsibility to shareholders, a short-term focus solely on the markets can cloud the decision-making of even the most well-intentioned leaders, who then justify all sorts of behavior by claiming that maximizing shareholder value is their single most important duty. That is why they pull the trigger on layoffs and cutbacks the instant revenues or profits slow, or just threaten to slow.

If executives and their boards are hyper-focused on keeping the stock price at the maximum multiple, it can be dangerous. Although that type of tunnel vision can lead to short-term financial gain for both shareholders and executives, if it influences their every decision, I believe it will threaten the long-term success of their franchises.

Meanwhile, one of the most enduring truisms of business, dating back to the beginning of the 20th century, is "the customer is always right." This means that we must listen to our customers intently to understand their problems. It does not necessarily mean, though, that companies must adapt their business development strategy, service and support apparatus, product development, and staffing plans based on the closest congruence with customers' needs and desires.

My 40 years at NetScout have taught me, and I strongly believe, both these attitudes can be counterproductive.

Enterprises that operate this way may have their priorities backwards. Why? Because everything depends on those same employees whom some companies treat as so expendable. How can a company expect deep loyalty from employees—in exchange for a mere paycheck—when they do not offer that same loyalty in return? Loyalty is a two-way street.

Developing that kind of mutual loyalty is a lot more difficult than it sounds. No matter how kind-hearted you are, if as a company, your loyalty to your employees emerges only during a crisis—that is, only when it is tested—it will prove to be tardy and ineffectual, and it will end in betrayal. You must demonstrate that loyalty long before things go bad.

What do I mean by that? If employee cutbacks are to be your absolute last resort—when you are out of other options to save the company—then you must prepare for that eventuality years ahead of time.

You need always to recruit and hire intelligently and sparingly. Does that mean that during boom times you and your employees may be burdened with extra work? Yes. But it also means that during tough times you will not be forced to betray that trust. Employees who trust their employers to have their best interests in mind return that attitude and redouble their efforts to make that employer survive and succeed. Keeping the communication lines open from the top down helps everyone feel they understand the vision and direction for a company, and the more they hear the more they want to participate in its success.

It is not always easy. The dot-com crash and the subsequent economic downturn from 2001 to 2005, along with a change in our relationship with our largest indirect channel partner, threatened to sink our company. Navigating a rebuild of our technology and sales channels, at a time when customers and prospects were focused on their own survival, was a daunting task. Fortunately, we had the cash to weather a protracted downturn and some patient shareholders and a board that shared our long-term views of the opportunities we saw.

So, at NetScout we made an extraordinary effort to keep our employees, by cutting costs everywhere else first. They, too, sacrificed a lot, including deferring any raises for multiple years. But we executed our plan and managed to save every job in the company.

Was it worth it? Absolutely. We continued to innovate, and we came out of the recession stronger than our competitors, who had weakened themselves through project cutbacks and layoffs and, in the process, lost the capacity to react quickly to the needs of their customers and to innovate solutions. Just as important, our employees repaid our trust with an era of productivity that propelled us to new heights. Because of that, we were able to double down on our investments during a very tough time, when our competitors were being cautious.

That was just the obvious impact. What was less obvious was the loyalty we built. Yes, our attrition rate through those tough years was low and, to be sure, the hiring climate at that time aided us. However, after the recession, when the job market was hot, our attrition rate remained extremely low. We stuck with our employees during tough times, and they in turn stuck with us during the good times, even when recruiters called offering higher salaries or better rewards.

NetScout has always dealt with balancing the needs of the company with the needs of employees in a unique way designed to maximize benefits for both. Take for example our compensation philosophy. We purposely keep base compensation to an average industry level but more than counteract the impact of base compensation with incentive and benefit programs that are very high relative to the rest of the industry. This has given us a level of flexibility that enables us to absorb the ebb and flow of industry boom and bust times with minimal impact to our employees, and our corporate bottom line. The decision of which economic levers to build into our budget and why were the direct result of applying the 5% Rule, and that decision has stood the test of time for more than three decades. We embraced the idea of "short-term pain for long-term gain" in the formation of our compensation philosophy, and we have seen it play out to the benefit of our employees and our company time and time again. With every economic recession, we all sacrificed, and the pain came in the form of salary freezes, lower bonuses (if any), lower revenue and profits, and a depressed stock price. But the gains invariably followed and far outweighed the sacrifices. They came in the form of innovation, market acceptance, top-line, and bottom-line growth, an eventually rising stock price, and enduring loyalty.

We did lose some employees to those recruiters, but we have seen a particularly telling phenomenon: many who left returned. Enough so that we even created an official recognition, the Boomerang Award, for the employee who has returned in the shortest time each year.

One recipient, who had been part of our team for a few years through the bleakest of times, gave his notice soon after the market improved. A larger, more established company had lured him away with a potentially higher compensation offer. We were surprised and disappointed that he left, because he was a talented individual who enjoyed his role, the people he worked with, and the corporate culture he helped perpetuate. Fortunately, we were able to quickly fill the vacancy he created.

A few months month later, he returned to us, saying, "I made a terrible mistake." Even though he had already sacrificed his unvested stock options and the only suitable opening we had available at the time was a lesser job, he still chose to return.

As I write this, many of these boomerangs are blooming and contributing to the success of NetScout, and they bring a unique perspective when training others to be genuine providers of our solutions. Although some companies may refuse to welcome back an employee who has left, we understand that former employees know our company and its culture, they are well trained and highly productive, they have a solid perspective about our direction, and they know we will listen to their "outsider" perspectives about growth and process changes as well. That is why, in many cases, we welcome them back.

Loyalty pays off in other ways as well. An obvious one is morale. We regularly conduct employee engagement surveys, like many other companies, partly to measure employee happiness year-over-year. We get a 90% response rate for most of these surveys. The 50 or so questions include a diverse collection of topics ranging from opinions about the roles the executive team and I play inside and outside of the company, to questions about how rapidly we integrate their contributions into an innovation or process, to questions about the quality of their life on the job.

What I find particularly satisfying is that, on questions related to company culture and value systems, we will see close to a 100% satisfaction rating. That is from people who have worked at NetScout for just a year, from people who have been here for 10 to 20 years, and from people who have just arrived from a new acquisition, regardless of the geographical location. This means that the company is doing its job well, on a consistent basis, when it comes to employee recognition and appreciation. If one of those measures should be dropped, it will not be the employees' fault, but mine and management's.

Two stories from NetScout's history capture the importance of mutual loyalty. About 2005, during tough times, we received an acquisition offer. Our stock price had dropped into the single digits, and the offer represented a potentially reasonable but not overly compelling premium to the current stock price. One of our late-stage investors, prior to the IPO (initial public offering), was anxious to sell. He told us, "I know we can stretch that offer a little higher."

Coincidentally, he envisioned a takeout price that would match what he had paid for our stock when he had invested. He said, "Things have not been going well at our firm, and we should go for it."

At that time, my cofounder and I were the two largest individual shareholders in the company, with a very low-cost basis. This meant that we would see the largest pay benefit from selling the company, and many of our employees, with much smaller equity stakes and a higher cost basis, would not reap much, if any, reward. Our institutional shareholder base was mixed, with long-term holders who may have incurred losses and some new entrants who might be satisfied with the short-term gain. More important, my cofounder and I agreed that this price did not represent true value for our assets and technology. Better yet, we made this case to the rest of the board, and they agreed, and we stayed independent.

Today, after being a public company for over two decades, NetScout holdings are distributed differently. Through dilution of founder holdings, through public offerings, issuing stocks for financial acquisitions, and stock awards to our employees, I now own less than 5% of the company, versus 50% when I cofounded NetScout. Thanks to our employee efforts, the company has become much more valuable, and the pool of potential buyers out there is smaller than it was when we received that buyout offer. And my shares, despite being just a fraction of my original holdings, are worth much more. In fact, their value has increased 25 to 50 times what it was, though my percentage of ownership has been reduced by 10 times. More important, in the process, we have created more than 50 millionaires at NetScout so far.

My dream is to create another 500 millionaires over the next five years. Just as important, today every employee at NetScout is also a shareholder, unless they are in a country where they are not allowed to own shares, in which case we compensate them with a cash equivalent. That fact is fundamental to creating a sense of ownership and loyalty.

As a founder or a CEO, I believe that your main goal should be to build a viable company, and the best way to do that is to get as many of your employees as possible involved as shareholders. Most employees are not hired because they fully understand how to build the company, or because they can structure or manage multiple functional areas, or because they know how to pursue an exit strategy. But they do understand that the value of their stock is related to the success of the company, and that the more productive they are, the more likely that ownership is going to grow in value. Ultimately, that is the one thing they need to know.

The second story involves a small company we had bought in Europe. After five years, we realized that the acquisition was not working out. The operation was no longer aligned with the company direction. It was fading fast, and to be masters of our destiny, rather than let events take their course, we decided to close the operation. Shutting down an operation is always painful, but shutting down an office in another country is exceptionally so, because there may be fewer opportunities to transfer employees to new positions in other locations.

From the beginning of that transition, we were resolved to do things right. We did not hide the plan from employees at the office, then dropped the unwelcome news on them at the last minute. Rather, we let them know as soon as we could, and we went to great lengths to help the employees find new jobs, offering some opportunities for relocation or equitable severance packages. As one of our vice presidents assured me, "I am going to follow your philosophy and values as we implement this transition."

You never know how things will work out when individuals are told their positions are no longer necessary. They can harbor bitterness and resentment, even if they understand intellectually why the changes are happening. So, it was with great satisfaction that soon after the closure was completed, I received a note from the person in charge of the office that we were closing. He told me how good he had felt through the entire process. Despite being written on his last day on the job, the letter was full of gratitude and praise for how well he and his staff had been treated. He said he felt like part of a family he could reach out to and call on throughout the rest of his career.

I cherish that note as a true testament to the 5% Rule and Lean But Not Mean in action. It is easy to earn respect when you are delivering good news. The real test of your value system—and the quality of your corporate culture—is whether you enjoy that same respect when you are delivering unwelcome news.

Does this seem like a lot of effort just to keep employees who, in the modern economy, are likely to move on eventually? Well, it is not. First, as our low voluntary attrition rate suggests, when you create the right culture, people are less likely to move on. Further, this premise is an excuse companies use to justify the Mean side of being Lean. In seeing their employees as expendable, these companies may miss what I think is one of the fundamental truths of modern business: You do not get revenue preservation without talent preservation.

Companies that are profligate with employee talent tend also to be so with the financial side of their businesses. Ironically, they do not appreciate what they are missing. Human capital, not financial capital, is today's scarcest resource. Therefore, the duty of each manager should have been to improve business performance and to increase returns on investments in human capital.

Now, let us not confuse loyalty to our employees with being an easy mark. We are not running a country club, but a tough-minded, aggressive business. At NetScout we have had some job applicants tell us that the reason they wanted to work for the company was that we "never fire anyone." We quickly disabuse them of that notion. Like many other companies, we do have performance plans and processes to make sure no one is taking advantage of the system. But for an employee who is not up to a particular job, instead of firing the person, we will try our best to help coach the employee or offer a second chance in another position. And we will never conduct a layoff unless all other options are exhausted, and never merely to artificially boost profits in the short term, because that would violate the mutual trust we cultivate with our employees.

Hopefully, you now understand why loyalty to employees is essential to business success. But you may be wondering: should "excited employees" really come before "satisfied customers"? We've all heard the maxim that the customer's happiness is all that matters, not to mention the obvious fact that revenues (and profits) come from customers, not employees.

My answer is that precedence in focus does not mean precedence in attention. Of course, you want happy and satisfied customers. But how do you get there? Is it even possible to achieve elevated levels of customer satisfaction with a workforce that is unhappy, indifferent, or suffering from low morale? I would argue that it is impossible, especially in the long term. You can spend all your time, money, and attention on customers, but if you cannot execute your actions effectively through your staff, your efforts will not amount to much. And a staff that is disaffected, disconnected, and disengaged is not likely to stay motivated over a long time.

However, when your employees are proud of their work and their company, they are willing to go that extra mile to make things right with customers, quickly spotting errors and rectifying mistakes. How much is the perception of superior attention and service delivered by motivated employees worth to your customers? I submit it can be deemed priceless.

Most of all, the reason employees come first is this: Customers come and go. That is inevitable. A longtime customer's employee you deal with may start working for a different company that has contracts with different vendors, or a new manager might decide to try a new vendor instead of renewing your contract, or you failed to anticipate a customer's needs, so they decided to look for services elsewhere.

For any number of reasons, customers will go, but when they do go, we want them to leave knowing that we did our best, and if they come back, we will do our best again. If a customer had a joyful experience while they were with you, there is a good chance that individual customer will one day come back to you. However, if a customer has been treated poorly, it is unlikely they will ever come back. A customer loss is disappointing; but a customer lost forever is painful.

Like all companies, NetScout dreads losing customers. To reduce attrition, we conduct continuous customer service training sessions with our employees. We provide our employees with masterful skills and a value system that has earned product and service quality awards from third parties.

Beyond training, though, it is our employee loyalty that creates a foundation for strong customer relationships. Employees with tenure have the experience to solve problems much faster and more efficiently, and they have the time to create long-lasting relationships with customers.

Further, when you practice loyalty to your employees, they mirror that loyalty to their customers. For example, two years ago, and from their own ingenuity, NetScout's marketing team created "Guardians of the Connected World," a broad, multidimensional leadership initiative. The philosophy of the Guardians rests on two postulates. First, our company's mission is to monitor the performance and security of corporate networks and everything else connected in the digital world. Second, as everything becomes increasingly connected, a whole new set of cybersecurity and performance problems have emerged. As the industry leader, finding solutions to those problems will be a particular challenge for NetScout and for our customers.

Hence, the Guardians: a corporate guideline that establishes our loyalty and our commitment to assume responsibility for solving some of the toughest problems of the connected world out of a sense of duty to our industry. This is not to say that we are a charity or a nonprofit, but as a for-profit company, we consider ourselves in the business of public service. Once again this is an argument for putting employees first. Who but enthusiastic, optimistic, and committed employees would create an initiative like the Guardians of the Connected World? Our customers benefit from the dual sense of pride and responsibility at the heart of this mission. The result of prioritizing employee enthusiasm is increased customer satisfaction.

At NetScout we have turned the traditional model upside-down, giving precedence to our employees, followed by our customers. In the preceding pages, I have tried to make the case that this reorientation produces higher customer satisfaction and truly delivers on the old maxim, "the customer comes first."

But we've yet to address the third variable in this equation: shareholders. Over the last 50 years, businesses around the world, particularly in the United States, have shifted from a customer focus to a near-obsession with shareholder satisfaction. Indeed, many public companies seem to operate with one eye—or both eyes—on their stock prices. Once that happens, this orientation informs their every action, shifting businesses away from a strategy of long-term, stable growth, such as creating enduring improvements in company value to one of short-term, even quarterly, increases in the value of the stock, creating quick, temporary jumps in the stock price rather than long-lasting shareholder value.

In my opinion, everyone agrees that this is not a salutary trend because it can distort company operations, add volatility to the economy, and give an advantage to international competitors with cultures that encourage taking the long view. Yet the economic system is increasingly oriented toward this way of doing business.

Now, when public companies fail to achieve short-term goals, the market reaction is swift and severe. Stock prices crater, soon followed by shareholder class action lawsuits. Activists step in to press management to change the capital structure, cost structure, or strategic direction (sometimes all three), and leveraged buyout experts hover, waiting to snatch up a bargain.

Given all of that, why would a company today not give first priority to its shareholders? This helps explain why the number of US publicly traded companies continues to shrink.

No company that cares about its long-term existence, much less its long-term success, can afford to live just quarter-to-quarter. Even more—and I believe this firmly—the only way truly to reward shareholders is to turn your eyes away from the stock ticker and focus on making your company successful. Counterintuitively, focusing on your employees first, and your customers second, will lead to shareholder rewards—and this is the only integral way to make all three constituents happy.

We have just looked at how prioritizing employees helps customers. Now I am going to make the same claim about shareholders: giving priority to employees and customers is the best way to help shareholders, by delivering long-term value. Remember that precedence in focus does not mean precedence in attention.

Taking a long-term strategy—and not worrying about stock price fluctuations—may sound good in principle. But in practice, in an economy that punishes stability over short-term gains, it can be exceedingly difficult to implement. One way to do it is, once again, to focus on employees. Give them stock, in the form of an employee stock ownership program and an employee stock purchase program.

Making employees into shareholders has all sorts of positive effects. Not only does it improve morale, but it also gives those employees a stake in the company's success and aligns their incentives with outside investors. But just as important for our current discussion, it creates a body of shareholders with a long-term orientation that can serve as a partial and symbolic counterbalance to the stock flippers' minute-by-minute gyrations of the stock price.

That is only the start. The success of this strategy comes down to education. It used to be that large public corporations were expected to pay annual dividends to their shareholders. The founding firms of the electronics industry changed all of that, preferring instead to reinvest their profits back into R&D to make the company even more competitive and the stock more valuable. Look at Apple, Microsoft, Cisco, and others today. Those smaller technology innovators thrived, and over multiple decades they grew large enough to begin paying dividends themselves.

The same is true now regarding long-term business thinking. In the short-term it may be more expensive to obtain capital if you announce that you are focused on long-term versus short-term value. But in the long term, if the stock market is educated to understand that your thinking will build a healthier and a more successful company, it will incorporate that understanding into your valuation.

That said, there is one immensely powerful constituency close to home, who may raise questions about this change in perspective: the board of directors. Their fiduciary responsibility, of course, is to represent the interests of shareholders—that is, the owners—of the company. That gives them, by law, enormous power over the company's direction. Moreover, given recent legal cases that add both to their responsibilities and their legal vulnerabilities, they understandably are more concerned than ever about maximizing shareholder values.

There are two answers to this dilemma. The first is that, from the start, you need to build a board that understands the importance and benefits of long-term company success that is dedicated to helping you get there and that shares your value system.

The second is, once again, education. Directors typically are very bright, successful people. That is why they are on your board. But they also dealt with the short-term environment and pressures of modern business. You need to make sure that they have ratified the company's strategy and vision, and that they have a means to assess progress.

New board members will also need to be educated about your successful record of accomplishment and how your business philosophy contributed toward that success. Then they will understand that if you do not have satisfied customers and excited employees, you may still see some short-term benefits in your stock price, but they will not last long. They will also understand that they, as well as the management team, are really fulfilling their fiduciary responsibilities to company shareholders by supporting a company strategy and business philosophy that focuses on long-term, sustained growth.

Loyalty to and from employees, customers, and shareholders is at the heart of the 5% Rule—and the only path to becoming a Lean But Not Mean company. The payback is excited employees who are cultivating satisfied customers and delivering more revenue and profits, which is, of course, bound to please shareholders.

The result, when done right, is an ever-upward virtuous spiral of perpetual success.

3

Trust Is the Ultimate Empowerment
The Decisive Factor

Trust is the soul of business, and a company culture built on trust is naturally both Lean and Not Mean. This chapter will explain why.

The title of this chapter may sound at best like a cliché and at worst like an anachronism, an attitude of an older, simpler time. Who talks about trust anymore, especially in a world in which many employees are nomads in perennial search of the next excellent job offer, and customers switch their product loyalties with a keystroke? But my purpose in this chapter is to advocate for trust. The idea of trust is, in fact, not obsolete; it is an idea so forgotten that it is almost new.

Trust your employees and partners by default, until proven otherwise—this is the basic rule by which we have tried to run our business at NetScout. Of course, trust builds over time, but on day one, we must begin with trust. Let us see how this works mathematically, assuming Trust increases by N every day, and is X on Day 1:

[Trust on Day 1] = X

[Trust on Day 2] = [Trust on Day 1] times N

[Trust on Day 1000] = [Trust on Day 999] times N

And so on . . .

In other words, trust multiplies and compounds. So, what should be the value of X or [Trust on Day 1]? As high as possible. By comparison, zero gives you no foundation for building continuous trust over time.

Yet, for many companies in our industry, trust starts at zero. Management often distrusts employees and vice versa. Investors look suspiciously at company directors, and those directors often assume that investors are waiting to betray them without a hint of provocation. Many customers assume they are being lied to, retailers think that distributors are cheating them, and manufacturers suspect that their suppliers and distributors are playing them fast and loose.

Ours is not an age built on universal trust. Yet, as any student of business history will tell you, the greatest companies have always shown high levels of trust between all stakeholders.

There are good reasons for this. For example, the best way to maximize profits is to create trusted, long-lasting relationships with customers, rather than paying the cost of new customer acquisition and training. Employees who trust their employers to treat them well—pay them a fair wage, avoid endless layoffs, and let them share in the company's success—tend to have higher morale, productivity, and commitment to the company.

So, how do you establish a good threshold of trust on day one, when a new employee has just joined the company? It begins during the interview process. That is where you first establish trust—in how you treat the interviewee, and their responses, with respect. That respect should extend throughout their employment, even to how you treat their departure someday.

One of the classic examples of trust-based success is Hewlett-Packard Co., circa 1956 to 1974. Thanks to their experiences in World War II, in the economic expansion that followed, and in the tech boom of the 1950s, the founders of Hewlett-Packard, Bill Hewlett and Dave Packard, determined that the only way to run their company successfully—that is, in a way that would be both adaptive and perpetually innovative—was to set general corporate objectives, then to trust the company's growing army of employees to figure out all of the nuances of achieving those objectives.

During their early days, Hewlett and Packard reinforced this trust—this belief that employees will reciprocate effective treatment with hard work and loyalty—by sharing ownership of the company with employees via profit sharing, stock purchase programs, and stock options. They further exhibited that trust by implementing a whole raft of revolutionary workplace innovations, including flextime, morning and afternoon snack breaks, tuition repayments, casual Fridays, management by walking around, their famous Friday beer parties, and many more. The company treated employees as adults in command of their own lives, not as ciphers on an organization chart.

This philosophy of management came to be known as *the HP Way* and was studied for a long time. Why? Because of its astonishing results: Through those years, researchers surveyed HP's employees and consistently found the highest levels of employee morale, loyalty, and dedication ever recorded by a large company.

This alone would be impressive enough. But during this period, HP was also one of the most innovative companies of all time, entering and dominating one market after another with breakthrough products in test and measurement instruments, minicomputers, calculators, medical devices, and a host of other products.

In short: As the HP example teaches us, trust works in business. It is the ultimate means to empower employees to work at the highest levels of their abilities. We have a half-century of proof that it works. And yet, in spite of all of that, too few companies base their value systems on it. Why?

The simple answer is that trust is hard. Trust goes against the accepted culture of many modern businesses. Most corporations are hierarchies of power. As you climb the organization chart, you accumulate ever more power, until at the top, as CEO, you have the greatest amount of power over the daily operation of the company. Having spent years—decades even— climbing to the top of the heap, why would you want to surrender this power?

Delegating authority is one thing—you must do that once your organization grows larger than a couple dozen employees. But entrusting others to operate autonomously, empowering them to make key decisions in the context of company's strategy, value system, and philosophy? That is another thing altogether. That takes both courage and an elevated level of belief in your subordinates. Such a combination of traits is rare, even—especially—among top executives, which helps explain why so few of the best-run companies can maintain a trust culture from one generation of leadership to the next.

And yet, to my mind, trust—driving power down through the hierarchy—is the fastest and most rewarding path to building an enormously successful company, one that is innovative, adaptive, structurally strong, highly efficient, and filled with happy and motivated employees. My reasons for believing this are not romantic, but entirely pragmatic: Trust lies at the very heart of the 5% Rule.

More than ever, business now moves at a breakneck pace—one that grows faster by the year, which means that business decision-making must be at least as fast. In practice, there is less time for that decision-making to move up through a multilevel organization to reach the person with the power to make a final decision, and then back down to the person who must execute that decision.

Great business leaders, such as Hewlett and Packard, soon come to the realization that the only way to accelerate decision-making to the speed of the modern economy is to tighten that loop, investing in the person who needs to execute with the power to do so.

Thus, one of my pragmatic reasons for cultivating a trust environment in our company (and practicing it myself) is that trust is a powerful time-saver. Not only are decision cycles faster throughout the organization but also, speaking personally, not having to worry about checking everyone's work once I have done my part at the beginning is a tremendous relief.

At NetScout, I place considerable trust, via the 5% Rule, in people when it comes to operations and execution. If you are a trusted employee, with the authorization to issue a $1 million check, and you have initialed a check request, then I will sign and endorse that check without hesitation. Here trust not only saves time but it also means a lot to the person who requested my signature. They have shown themselves to be responsible; why should I constantly question that responsibility?

I do, however, clearly draw a line between operational and strategic decisions. For the latter, you are still trusted, but I must always reserve the right to oversee those decisions. That is my job.

When you combine the time savings, the increase in productivity, and the motivation that comes from your employees feeling trusted and respected, something magical happens.

I call it *the management multiplier effect*. If, as a leader or manager, you do not have to double-check your subordinates' every decision, you can instead concentrate on what else needs to be done to make the company more competitive or to improve your bottom line—thus multiplying your impact. This leads to a Lean decision-making culture, one which delivers meaningful results in a short time and consistently, indirectly eliminating costs and contributing to the bottom line. This is one of the most powerful manifestations of the 5% Rule.

Imagine a highly productive, adaptive company that brings together the combined intellectual capital of its workforce, fosters independence in its employees, and enjoys the tightest possible decision cycles. One that is led by executives who can devote their attention to the larger issues of strategy, rather than spending their time dealing with tactics.

Who would not want a company like that?

Strategic Retention

I think that most companies that focus on employee retention focus on what happens after an employee is hired—work satisfaction, salary, rewards, career development, and all the other things that make an employee content in their job. A lost employee is a loss of talent and experience, and the latter is difficult to replace.

I am not going to diminish the importance of that—after all, it is critical to the Lean But Not Mean philosophy that employee satisfaction has top priority—but I am also convinced that the process of employee retention begins even before that employee is hired. Retention is a feature of the 5% Rule, not least because you do not want to lose a team member during executing the initiative.

To my mind, the definition of *employee talent* is not just people who are good, but people who are good and want to be at NetScout. Those are the people we want to hire, and once they are hired, we want to make sure they do not want to leave. If, from day one, or even after some time, they really do not want to be here, then no reward or benefit will convince them to stay.

We learned this lesson the hard way. Like many tech companies, during the dot-com bubble we were so desperate for talent that we hired fast and with little consideration of the unique contribution the person could add to the rich culture we were trying to build. In other words, we just looked at the skills listed in their résumé and not the values they bring with them. This was a mistake. As the boom continued, we lost as many people as we hired, creating confusion and chaos in the company, even as we struggled to keep up with exploding demand.

Then the crash came and passed, and we were still standing. Many of those employees who had left during the economic good times wanted to come back to NetScout during the economic bad times, but few were rehired. However, those who chose to stay through the boom, often eschewing offers from other companies, remain with the company 10 to 15 years later. These are some of NetScout's biggest champions.

Out of this experience, we developed our own process for hiring new people, beginning with a rule that, in some departments, we try to avoid using recruiters or headhunters to find new talent. Instead, many of our new hires come to us through word-of-mouth—by current NetScout employees, former NetScout employees, and surprisingly often, by our customers. Obviously, we vet these applicants, but the biggest confirmation that someone is meant to be a Guardian of the Connected World is that someone who already knows our values and culture of trust can attest to them. If they trust the person, then we are more likely to trust that person, too. This hiring practice enables the new employee to start work with that prominent level of trust on day one.

Personally, I like this process because, as I am the first to admit, I am not a great interviewer. I know that I am not going to be able to plumb the soul of a new job applicant during an interview.

But I can be a particularly good salesperson. So, if an applicant comes before me with the company's seal of approval after the standard interview process, then I can focus on what I do best: getting them to fall in love with NetScout, while establishing a threshold of trust on day one.

Trust as Simplifier

There is yet another pragmatic reason for creating a culture of trust: Lack of trust forces redundancy—in operations and, even more, in employees. If you do not trust lower-level employees to do their jobs, you not only have to increase their numbers to be sure the work gets done but also increase the number of supervisors overseeing their work. This redundancy creeps right up the organization chart to the CEO. Obviously, you cannot have two of them, but you will have to beef up the ranks right below the CEO to take over all those small tasks to free the boss to focus on strategy and other big picture challenges.

What I am describing here is the antithesis of a Lean organization. Moreover, when a company bloated with redundancies hits a rough patch, it inevitably must also become Mean. When businesses tank, such companies find not only that they must initiate layoffs but also that they cannot lay off employees fast enough. The result? The employees who survive the cuts are left depressed and suffering low morale, and they are suffering these consequences not because of changes in the business environment, but because the company leadership did not trust them.

Would it not be better just to trust your employees from the start? Not only will they be more productive and motivated during the good times, but when the business cycle makes its inevitable turn, you will be better equipped to get through the tough time, emerging from it Lean, happy, and ready to take advantage of the next economic upswing.

Building Trust

It is important to note that a culture of trust is not something you can impose on either an organization or any of the individuals within it. You must start small, with growing degrees of trust-driven empowerment, and then systematically work your way toward ever-greater autonomy for your employees at all levels.

Over the years I have developed some rules about this process that I would like to share with you:

- Trust is built by the individual. It is not granted by their title. That administrative assistant in accounting may have shown that they deserve full autonomy in business dealings and decisions, while their boss may not be ready yet for that kind of independence. You need to look past job title, seniority, education level, or any other factor and be clear-eyed about who deserves their independence.

- Trust includes promoting employees before they may feel ready for their new role, believing, based on their past performance, that they will rise to the occasion and earn the power that comes with the position.

- Never outsource your vision. Learn to trust your own judgment. You are in your position because you deserve it. Other people trust you to do the job; you in turn should trust that they have made the right decision.

- Real trust cannot be shaken easily. Even in a trust-based corporate culture, people will still make mistakes. They will still delude themselves, and they occasionally will lapse into distrusting each other. That is not a sign of a failure of this philosophy, but rather of human nature. You need to believe that your employees want to trust each other, and they want to be trustworthy themselves. In my experience that is, in fact, the case. Your patience will always be rewarded.

- Untrustworthy people will not last long in a trust-based culture. A final pragmatic reason for a trust-based company culture is that it quickly throws cases of untrustworthiness into sharp relief. A weakness of trusting companies is that they are uniquely vulnerable to devious and untrustworthy employees, who can run roughshod through the organization, taking advantage of one person after another. Should such an individual emerge, they must be dealt with swiftly. There should be no second chances—after all, your employees trust the company to protect them. The good news is that, with time, the company will become increasingly resistant to these individuals as it focuses on recruiting like-minded employees.

- Trust is the ultimate empowerment. We are back to where we began. *Empowerment* is an overused word in modern corporate life, and like most overworked terms it seems to have grown many definitions. Too often, *empowerment* is little more than a term used to give people a false belief that they have control over their situations, when in fact that control is being tightly monitored by others.

True empowerment is the ability to act in accordance with your own judgment and experience, with the minimum of oversight. When every decision you make is questioned, that is not empowerment. True empowerment does not demand that you do everything right or your power will be revoked. Nor can true empowerment be taken away whenever an authority figure gets nervous or apprehensive. True empowerment recognizes that you are human and will make mistakes, but it also trusts you to do the best job possible.

Though I understand why, I am still astounded by how many companies do not establish and cultivate trust-based cultures. Sure, it is challenging, even counterintuitive. As much trust as such a culture expects from employees, it demands even more from senior management. Yet, as difficult as it may be for a company to implement and maintain a culture of trust, the return far outweighs the cost.

Again, who does not want a company of happy, highly productive employees comfortable in operating on their own that can respond quickly to any challenge, and adapt just as fast to any change, good or bad?

Would you look forward to going to work each morning at that company?

4

Transparency in Practice
It's Not Just a Buzzword

Much has been made, in recent years, about the need for transparency within organizations.

I half-heartedly disagree.

Let me explain. According to some management experts, transparency about everything from company strategy to employee compensation is a positive force because it increases trust and removes barriers to action and to effective teamwork.

Some companies have experimented with this business ideology, with decidedly mixed results. The reality of transparency is a lot messier—and sometimes a lot more damaging—than the dream. Experience, some of it painful, has taught me that transparency is good, but you need to be careful not to share everything. My rule is to share with others what they need to know before they ask for it. This is a key component of a Lean But Not Mean culture.

The first pitfall of full transparency is human nature. We're not that comfortable with full exposure. We do not always take it well when we learn that the employee sitting across from us, doing the same job as us, is earning 10% more than us. No amount of explanation—the person's seniority, training, education, or superior negotiating skills during the hiring process—is going to mollify us.

Similarly, some people are better at keeping secrets, and other people could not keep a secret if their lives depended on it. The latter person may be a wonderful employee in every other way, but are you really going to share trade secrets, or your long-term business strategy, with that person? Not if you properly understand your fiduciary responsibility to company shareholders.

Conversely, although it is far simpler to make company operations opaque, in the long-term, internal operations will stop slowly if you do. Employees need to talk with each other and share actionable information if the company is going to move with the speed, efficiency, and decisiveness needed in this ultra-competitive global business world. So, what is the formula for optimal transparency?

As Clear as You Can Be

Let me note at this point that my objection to complete company transparency is not based on a gratuitous need to hide valuable information from employees. On the contrary, I think an organization, for the sake of efficiency, should be as transparent as it can be—safely. So how do you determine "safe" transparency?

Of course, you need to restrict access to some information because it could be damaging to morale or could lead to employee conflict, or because confidentiality is required legally, or because transparency could potentially compromise company secrets. But that is just half the story. There is another half, which I think is just as important.

In a quest to be open—that is, to not be accused of being secretive with employees—company management can go too far, engaging in oversharing. Burdening employees with too much unnecessary knowledge can lead to a loss of productivity.

Twenty-first century business life is deluged with data—from minute-by-minute records of internal operations to big data files and analytics about supply, retail channels, and customer purchasing behavior. True transparency would demand that you dump all this information on your employees. Would this help them? I would argue that this kind of oversharing—on them and on you—only leads to anxiety, confusion, and ambiguities within the organization. Rather than making the company more efficient and responsive, it just gums up the work.

Instead, I have developed a strategy of information transparency that works everywhere from software and hardware development to HR. It has three key tenets:

- Provide employees with the information they need to do their jobs, and no more. If they want more information, they can work for it, and that is usually enough to keep them from wasting their time searching for information they do not need.

- Let people know what information they can ask for—and make it available to them when they want or need it. But they must request it and justify why they need it to do their jobs effectively.

- Some things—including salaries and trade secrets, legally confidential information, or even details about a different department or business—need to be opaque. Keep them that way. Transparency of this kind of information only diminishes company productivity and efficiency.

When sharing information, your primary emphasis should be, once again, on the why? not on the what? or the how? In the modern corporation, employees need to know an awful lot of information, but not all the information. If we compromise those boundaries out of some romantic and foolhardy notion that all transparency is all good, or that "information needs to be free," in the end, we will do employees and our companies a disservice.

Instead, give information the privacy it deserves. No more and no less. The right information, provided proactively, will lead to higher productivity and, hence, Lean operations and better outcomes.

The Tie That Binds

Transparency may be the most challenging characteristic for a company to achieve, there being so many social and cultural impediments in the way to exposing everything from company decision-making to employee salaries. In addition, there can be logistical barriers to transparency. There may be organizational distance, as well as organizational diversity. A $1 billion multinational public corporation can have millions of stakeholders (not least shareholders), and internally it may have dozens of divisions, scores of sales offices in different countries, travel offices, corporate donations, internal education programs, employee publications, legal, facilities, and on and on—and all serving tens or even hundreds of thousands of employees.

This poses a profound challenge to your company's culture and internal communications. But for a company to operate at its greatest efficiency an underlying transparency is critical.

I believe the best way to achieve transparency in a company is to implement a culture of fairness at all levels, north-south as well as east-west. Choosing a culture of fairness right from the start creates a strong foundation of transparency for the company in the future. This makes all communications simpler, powerful, and easier, which is the ultimate goal of transparency. Coupling this with the 5% Rule can work to keep the organization, even when it is working independently, on the right path and with its eye on the prize. Meanwhile, it frees you to focus on the big decisions—like where the company goes next.

CHAPTER

5

Hierarchy of Purpose

Prioritizing Values

How do you create from nothing a company that can last a half-century, through good times and bad, recessions and booms, technological revolutions, and generations of customers? And how do you do it without laying off employees, betraying shareholders, or disappointing those customers by failing to keep up with the changing times?

By staying true to what you are, while holding no loyalty to past successes.

That is the hardest lesson for a company and its leaders to learn—it does not come easy—and conversely, it is too easy to forget under the press of daily business. It took my company—and me—a decade to learn the basics of this lesson and another 20 years to discover its details and nuances, much less execute on that understanding.

Today, it seems the accepted view that all a company needs is a "mission statement"—an anodyne sentence or two that captures the company's business, its competitive ambitions, and its dedication to being an enlightened employer. That's all nice, but how many companies live their mission statement, rather than using it as a publicity gesture posted on the wall in their lobby and on the first page of their stock prospectus?

Mission statements are often worthless because they fail in many ways. First, for all their generalities, they are usually limited in life span—even though they pretend to be immutable. Second, they are just as often more about product—ever-changeable—and less about enduring purpose. And third, they typically make claims about the company's underlying character and culture that have little evidence in actual practice.

But the biggest failure of most corporate mission statements is they have no teeth, that they are most often observed in the breech, because if the board of directors or the CEO—or ideally, the entire rank-and-file of the company—feel no compulsion to adhere to that statement, and there are no consequences for not doing so, it is rendered meaningless. It is extremely easy for top management to decide whether a temporary situation is too dire or an opportunity too good to stick to the mission statement's admonitions. And from that moment the mission statement, originally designed to define the company's long-term actions, becomes hollow.

Here is the reality, hard-earned over a half-century: A company's purpose is not a few sentences posted on a wall; rather, it is a hierarchy of values, strategies, and tactics, each coloring the other, and each with their own life span, duties, and attitudes. None can function on their own successfully over time—and yet all are in perpetual tension with each other. And, unfortunately, those responsible for adhering to that hierarchy are often lured, for temporary gain, to compromise them.

Learning Curve

Here is how I first came to understand this hierarchy of a company's purpose:

Values
   Purpose
      Vision
         Mission
            Products/Technology

You can read this pyramid in either direction: up and down or down and up. Presented as shown here, it is like a corporate food chain.

At the top, the source of everything in a company's story, the first mover, is **values**, that is, what do you bring to the company at its creation?

This is typically the contribution of the founder(s), and it precedes the creation of the enterprise. What beliefs, morals, and ethics do they bring to this entrepreneurial enterprise? What do they value? And what do they consider anathema to the operation of the company?

You might think these values do not really matter. Why couldn't a person heretofore unethical in their business or personal dealings create a company dedicated to fair and honest dealings?

Well, it's possible. That individual has had a conversion or epiphany and decided to now follow the straight path. But I have never seen it. Far more likely is that a founder will bring to the company their long-established value system and through day-to-day interaction with subordinates, customers, and investors stamp the company with those values, which in time will become the company culture.

Companies inevitably reflect in some important way the values of those who built them. That is why the values the company is built on are not only uphill from every other characteristic of that company but also the most enduring of that company's traits.

In great companies, those values remain defining from the first day of the company to, sometimes centuries later, the last day of its existence. That is why it is so crucial to start a company with the right team, and over time, hire leaders with the best character. Companies with great values have the greatest chance of long-term success.

Next on the pyramid is purpose, which for years was eclipsed by the more mystical term, *vision*. But as we live in an era of a proliferation of new business jargon, plain old purpose has made a (not) surprising comeback.

Purpose is what happens when values meet opportunity and are disciplined by "higher ambition." It is what your company does—not in terms of actions, but in consequences. You may change the operations of your company over the course of the decades—look at IBM: from office equipment to corporate data processing to consumer computing to corporate services—but you change your larger purpose at your peril.

It follows that your purpose must be congruent with your values—and it must define all the steps in the hierarchy that follow. Regarding "higher ambition"—that phrase has too often come to mean (to the rue of many companies) "let's attach ourselves to the latest social trends to make us look good and to insulate us from criticism about our business dealings."

That is public relations, not honest and ethical business. True "higher ambition" is the commitment of taking only those actions that are congruent with the company's values. And as one of those values is usually "treating stakeholders equally and honestly," picking sides to influence their belief systems is always a mistake because those sides continuously change over time.

A company's purpose is what its mission statement purports to be: a statement of its enduring values as reflected in the company's goals of having a positive and material effect on humankind, and as made manifest in its market space and its value to customers.

Can that be done in a sentence or two? Absolutely. But it takes time to create. And it is what the company is and what it stands for—it should never be a marketing pitch.

One of the most interesting new models of purpose (and, in fact, it has helped bring back the term) is massive transformative purpose (MTP), first promoted by Salim Ismail, Peter H. Diamandis, and Michael S. Malone in their book *Exponential Organizations 2.0* (Ethos Collective, 2023). MTPs are the ultimate in higher ambition—indeed, they are impossible. But that is the point. They establish a purpose for the enterprise, a quest, that guides and disciplines the organization and its employees (even its stakeholders) to a single-minded quest to change the world in some important and valuable way.

In the MTP model, when you join a company, you adopt its vision and values—and, once internalized, it guides all your actions and decisions without outside control. In theory, it keeps you and everyone else in the company, right up to the C-suite, from making a foolish or misguided choice because you will know instantly that it is not "what we do" as defined by the MTP.

How big should an MTP be? Excessively big. NASA's MTP is to explore and inhabit the universe, Bill Gates's is to end malaria, Google's is to control and make accessible all the world's information. It may seem silly for some little nongovernmental organization to announce that it intends to end world hunger—but why not? Look at what has been accomplished by companies pursuing their impossible visions.

The challenge with an MTP is devising one. It may seem absurdly arrogant to announce, "We will make earth's poles inhabitable" or "We will cure diabetes" or "We will live on Europa." But those are kinds of flights of ambition needed for a good MTP.

MTP sounds good in theory, but it is only for the most ambitious companies and the best run. As with most things, real life always tempers theory. Not every enterprise can, or should, set out to change the world. But most can find a much greater purpose than the unimaginative and limiting one they have now.

More pragmatically, an MTP does have a practical purpose. As a quest, it perpetually motivates employees, making the often-dreary life at work exciting and with a real purpose. Even the lowest-level employee knows they are pursuing something great and important. During tough times (and good) that alone may convince your employees to stick with you.

Whatever size your mission turns out to be, take the time to find your true purpose for being in business.

Purpose, as the next step down on our hierarchy, should prove as durable as values. The only difference is that you found your company's purpose through your values—and, as an individual, those values will stay with you long after you leave.

Vision is the complex scenario the company develops as it imagines itself moving forward through time, executing its purpose. This vision may include how it furthers funding, the expansion of its markets to the larger world, the locations of new facilities, added customer services, new product development, community relations and other changes and adaptations as the company matures, expands, and searches for new markets.

In one respect, the company's vision can be seen as a road map into the future, complete with mileposts, that achieved will require new actions or changes (such as an initial public offering, or entry into the consumer market, or the construction of new facilities).

The company vision of its future can become detailed and elaborate—but beware the straitjacket of too much fidelity to the plan. The world is ever-changing and notoriously unpredictable, and plans must adapt to those changes. The dreams of a 5-year-old company can be quite different from a 40-year-old company. So do not be nostalgic for the good old days; think of the future as being even brighter.

Mission is often confused with vision, but they are very distinct phenomena. Purpose is why the company exists and it takes the perspective of consequences. Mission is how the company plans to execute that purpose to achieve the desired results (revenues, profits, market share, reputation, goodwill, customer loyalty, employee job security).

Mission can be seen as the combination of two processes—again, in modern jargon, blue ocean, and moonshot.

The notion behind blue ocean is that the most successful and defensible business strategy is to not compete with your competitors. Tremendously successful companies always construct their own unique markets, fill them with innovative products that are continuously being upgraded and differentiated away from any new market entries, and implement a pricing model that keeps those products the inevitable customer choice.

The greatest example of a blue ocean strategy in our time was the Steve Jobs–era Apple, which created five entirely new, multibillion-dollar markets, then owned them. But you can also find the successful implementation of mission at the early Google, Facebook, and others, which completely owned their markets.

Moonshots are big company initiatives. The name, of course, derives from the NASA programs of the 1960s. They were undertaken, under the order of President Kennedy, to not just put a man on the moon but also to leapfrog a competitor (the Soviet space program).

A corporate moonshot is similar in its goals. It is the mission made practical, and, at least in part, achievable. But it will not be easy. It will take a major commitment from every department in the company, as well as contributions from existing and future suppliers. And that commitment may take years.

That's the point: Moonshots are how ambitious companies escape the inertia of everyday business-as-usual, the risk aversion that can kill even the most successful companies.

Achieving a moonshot's goal can be transformative for a company, leaving competitors in the dust, creating a whole new industry that it instantly dominates, and making it a powerful recruiter for the best talent, who want to share in the success. A moonshot is the perfect vehicle to execute a blue ocean initiative. By definition, a moonshot is the best means to establish a new and unexploited market—and to do so with a fundamentally new product or service offering—by leapfrogging the competition into the future.

Similarly, a moonshot is a powerful tool to employ in hastening a company's ongoing pursuit of its purpose. But to do so, it must stay within the constraints of that purpose; otherwise, it will quickly destroy that Purpose—replacing it with something else (sowing confusion in the company and with its customers) or worse, nothing at all.

Products/technology are the realization of mission (and the ultimate manifestation of purpose). Products (and in that term I include technology, services, and other forms of company offerings for sale) are the shortest-lived of all the steps in our company hierarchy. Great products may last six decades in all their permutations and upgrades); mediocre products six years; failed products six months, or even six weeks.

That said, products are the key factor in a company's story. Without them, and the sales and profits they create, the company ceases to exist. Therefore, they are the point of contact with the outside world that fulfills the company's promise at all other levels of the hierarchy; they manifest its values, purpose, vision, and mission.

Products too have their own pair of internal mechanisms. In this case, they are, first, the manifestation of the enterprise's current strategy—its longer-term plan for growth and profitability, as well as for capturing new customers and market share, as well as satisfying the changing demand by current customers. And second, they are the implementation of tactics, the means—product innovation and design, applications, service and support, marketing, and sales—by which that demand is amplified and fulfilled.

For a company to survive and grow over the course of decades, even centuries, it must be excellent at each step of the hierarchy of purpose. And that is the paradox: How do you, in a rapidly changing world, adhere to the fixed standards of your values and your purpose, while pursuing your long-term vision, constantly updating, and modifying your mission and continuously introducing or upgrading your products to capture the latest shifts in demand, markets, and technology? How do you stand still and move at the breakneck pace of the modern world at the same time? It seems impossible—and yet we know it can be done. I feel as if my company has already been around forever—and it has, compared to the length of a typical career (mine)—but against the likes of companies such as Baretta and Bass Ale, which have held fast to their respective visions for centuries, we are but an adolescent company. They are proof that the dream is real; it can be done.

Real-Life Practice

I promised myself in drafting this book that I would faithfully adhere to real-life business as it is practiced and to pragmatic, practical wisdom that I had acquired over the years and wanted to share—and not to theory and philosophy that no reader realistically can put into practice. So, you've just read about the latter you are going to encounter in this book.

Still, I wanted to address these matters because they are especially important as the overall structure on which everything that follows can be attached to make your company an enduring success. And I am now going to finish this chapter by showing how, in real life, even this theoretical model can be put into practice.

First, it is important to note this is the ideal hierarchy of purpose for a commercial enterprise. In the real world, the process is a lot messier.

For example, these steps rarely occur in order and never as a complete model for implementation. We founded NetScout with a good sense of our own personal values, but we did not elucidate them as company values for a decade. But they have remained in place ever since.

Our ostensible purpose bounced around for the first few years of the company until we finally realized that all those data points described a common direction . . . and only then did we give it a title.

Mission was decided for us by the vagaries of competitive life in our corner of the tech world. It was in making company acquisitions that we were forced to truly define what we were doing (and not doing).

And products? They are evolving, as they should, even as I write this. We currently have three major product lines. The first two were created at a time when we still had not determined who we were. And we were lucky not to have gotten ourselves off track. It was our still-nebulous notion of our purpose that saved us.

Now every new product, and every new acquisition, must survive the gauntlet of fitting the template of our purpose, vision, and mission—or we walk away.

Along the way, we have also learned something else: that this hierarchy is not a pyramid—or even a hierarchy at all—but a dynamic. It is a constant interplay in which one step necessarily leads to the next. Some of those steps are permanent, or relatively so, but that does not mean they do not have immediate application when the process reaches their span of control. Moreover, at any given moment various parts of the company may be at different points in the process. That is how real-life business works.

So, instead of a food chain, NetScout now visualizes this (not-so) hierarchy in what we call a high-ambition (HA) map:

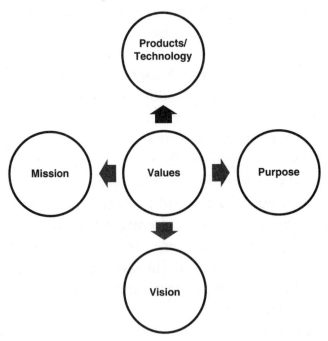

Note some key features. The first is that values, in all their forms, reside at the epicenter. This is proper for the one, inviolate, fixed, and permanent factor in a company's story. It is at the center of the action because it colors all other actions taking place around it. Unlike the other components, it influences but is not influenced by everything else. It provides the answer to the question that must be asked at every step along the way: Does this (product/action/decision) fit with who we are?

Note also that the other four factors in a company's identifying activities orbit values. Going clockwise, they replicate the levels of durability, from enduring purpose to vision, to mission, to ever-changing products/technology. But being in a circle, they are not constrained to only progress in a clockwise direction. If necessary, the direction can reverse—for example, a fundamentally new, market-creating, breakthrough technology may affect a product/technology and force a revision or reinterpretation of mission.

In fact, in the highly innovative, fast-moving competitive world within which my company operates, this kind of radical reassessment of our mission happens quite often. Since I began writing this, the business, academic, and political world has been upside down with the announcement of new AI tools that can duplicate human writing in an impressive way. The current talk is how many white-collar jobs it will replace. Meanwhile, surveys show that 40% of large companies in the United States believe that they will not be around a decade from now, thanks to technological change.

I am not saying that those fears are misplaced. Indeed, history shows that during major technological paradigm shifts, a lot of enterprises—even huge and famous ones—disappear, and sometimes with stunning speed. In many ways, this is the ultimate Mean management action: laying off thousands of employees, economically damaging whole communities, leaving millions of customers without service and support (and resale value), and saddling suppliers and retailers with vast inventories that can, at most, be written off.

Company executives may claim they were blindsided by change or the appearance of a new competitor. But the reality is that they did not do their job; they did not keep their eyes open. And they did not understand who they were as a company. And that left them unable to effectively respond to the latest threat.

They were not watching because they did not have the right vision to do so. They became complacent and without a larger purpose to compel them forward.

Putting It All Together

If you pursue long-term growth and success, your company needs to marshal all its resources—capital, people, supporters, technology—in the most efficient and powerful way to achieve that end. Zigzagging your way along, pursuing the latest interesting business opportunity, the newest obsession of one of your board members, that latest fad, you radically increase your odds of making a wrong turn and destroying yourself.

Yes, you need to be cognizant of outside competitive threats, especially the ones that seem to come out of nowhere; but this is where the 5% Rule can be used to help you stay focused on your business, not waste your intellectual capital, and to be able to respond quickly.

That means moving as fast as possible in a straight line toward your goal, and whenever possible, take risks—moonshots—to jump ahead. A circuitous business path, of being distracted by the latest fad or opportunity, is dangerous because it slows you down, enables your competitors to catch up, and it is expensive. For your company to survive for generations, you cannot afford to make those mistakes.

You need a clear direction—and that is best accomplished by applying the 5% Rule, with its combination of clear direction and rapid decision-making to the example high-ambition map.

With the 5% Rule and the HA map, you now have a model for successfully and rapidly navigating a straight path through the obstacles, both external and internal, that lie ahead. But that model will only work if you fill in each of those factors with facts adapted to your company's operations. If you cannot do that now, then you know what you need to do.

Do not expect the answers to come overnight—but keep in mind, until you can fill in all those blanks, your company's identity and operations are incomplete, and thus vulnerable.

The HA Map in Action

I will close by showing you how NetScout operationalizes its HA map. Note that we took the actual phrasing very seriously—appropriately so for titles that might last generations.

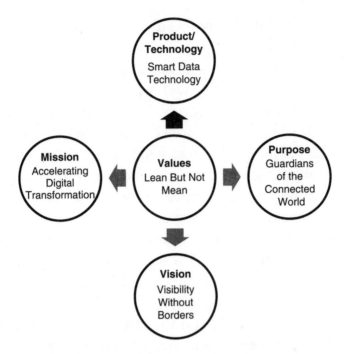

At the center, our core value philosophy is that we are a Lean But Not Mean company.

We have no MTP, but we most certainly do have far-reaching purpose, one that remains the same yet is constantly changing in its realization: we are the Guardians of the Connected World. The notions of duty and service found in the venerable word *guardians* is conscious; it reflects not only that the task is both sweeping and never-ending but also must be able to adapt to constantly changing tasks.

Our vision statement is that we provide our customers with the ability to investigate their operations in real time, regardless of platform. That is, we offer Visibility Without Borders. In other words, every decision we make must meet the criteria of enabling our customers to maintain full visibility and control of their infrastructure from every conceivable platform, from servers to smartphones.

What do we offer our customers? Our mission is to help them in Accelerating [their] Digital Transformation. Translation: We undertake perpetual digital transformation to empower our customers to complete control of their infrastructure.

And our current products/technology? They are characterized by our unique and patented technology called Smart Data, which has two meanings: first that the data we provide our customers is not raw but has been transformed into information that is useful and immediately applicable, and second that this transformed data enables users to make smart decisions via smarter analytics.

Finally, how do we accomplish this while operating under the 5% Rule? Here is an example of how we use the HA map to introduce new product solutions to our marketplace:

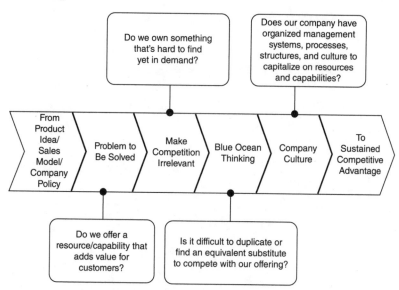

As part of our corporate culture, all employees from the top to the bottom of the organization have adopted these tenets and can explain them in depth. They protect these steps and know they can asset them even with their superiors. It is their company and, given our employment policies, they have every reason to expect to be here for their entire careers. NetScout's success is their success—and vice versa.

If you were asked to fill out this map with your company-appropriate titles and descriptions, could you, do it? If not, you should make completing that task a top priority. Your company's life could very well depend on it.

Building a Great Company

Implementing the 5% Rule

This section looks at the full panoply of an established company's operations and activities—from negotiations to mergers to price setting to employee advancement—and shows how the 5% Rule finds its place in all of them. One of the reasons that the 5% Rule is so universally applicable in the corporate world (and indeed, in nonprofits, the military, and government) is that it is not a rigidly enforced instrument, but rather an attitude, a process whose benefits accrue from shifting the key decision-making process to the leader at the very beginning of an initiative, then entrusting subordinates to execute on those decisions—without making major mid-course corrections—and only at the end having the leader return to finalize the deal

For example:

- Chapter 6, "Front-Loading Negotiations," talks about why it is so critical at the very start of a negotiation session to understand not only what is important to you but also to other side.

- Chapter 7, "Why Earn-Outs Are Bad for Acquisitions," talks about why it is important to spend quality time to understand not just a strategic fit but also a cultural and organizational fit, even before a letter of intent is signed and long before due diligence begins.

- Chapter 8, "Be a Problem-Solver, Not a Solution Provider," talks about why it is important to first drive a quick consensus on a crisp and unambiguous problem definition because it then directly drives a productive discussion with the entire team on potential solutions to that problem.

- Chapter 9, "Control the Timetable of Disruptions," talks about how and why to accelerate the timetable for disruption as soon as you sense that it is imminent.

- Chapter 10, "The Power of Being Different," talks about "difference" as a source of getting attention, because it gets the ear plugs out before you tell your story. It is also a more effective way to compete—you can't easily beat a very good basketball team, unless you can convince them to play football, which you know you are very good at.

- Chapter 11, "Put All Your Eggs in the Fewest Baskets," argues for taking risk by selecting the fewest options with the highest possibility of success, instead of too many options, which end up diluting the efforts; the popular phrase "don't put all your eggs in one basket" tells you what not to do versus what you should do.

- Chapter 12, "Don't Worry About Leaving Money on the Table," argues for always knowing what you need, or would be satisfied with, rather than "as much as possible"; knowing this at the beginning of an important negotiation and transaction makes the underlying process that more productive with the result of a win-win partnership.

- Chapter 13, "Communications Disconnects at the Top," talks about why it is so important how top-level management needs to be perfectly aligned before any communications to the lower levels of the organization; the senior leadership not only have to agree on the priorities of the business but also be aligned on the underlying reasons for each one of them.

- Chapter 14, "Primary and Secondary Skills," emphasizes why leadership skills are even more important in the second phase of an individual's career rather than domain-specific skills that are more important in the first phase. I further argue that the leadership skills, and hence the secondary skills, are directly proportional to the ability to successfully implement the 5% Rule at both the individual as well as the organization level.

This seem a radical way to lead an enterprise, but it is, in fact, a very conservative process. It forces you to make all the important decisions at the very beginning. That is, it makes you decide at the start just exactly what you want. It is the very embodiment of the 5%

Rule in the decision-making process because it doesn't allow you to deviate from that decision and thus escape most of the wastefulness—changing your mind later on, chasing another opportunity, wasteful company and employee resources that could have been used elsewhere, and, in the case of negotiations in mergers or employment contracts, leaving a bitter or unforgiving party on the other side of the table.

That it is attitudinal and not merely instrumental makes it so universal a process. In fact, without thinking, we use the 5% Rule constantly in our everyday lives. In almost everything we do we take a moment to decide on a strategy ("I'll stop by the bank first because it's on the way—and I'll need some cash at the drugstore . . .). We do this because it saves time and energy when we execute that plan over other more wasteful ones.

As you read the following chapters in this section, consider how your business model differs from this one—can you make a strong case that your business is superior in terms of speed, efficiency, at instilling loyalty in both your employees and customers? Now that you have been introduced to the 5% Rule, can you find it being practiced in any operation in your company— and would it work to map that program to every part of your enterprise? Would you trust your employees enough to let them execute an entire company initiative once you have given them your input at the start?

Finally, look ahead 20 years, 50 years even, in an ever-accelerating economy and with a society largely driven by AI, robotics, integration, and convergence, and even greater international competition. Will the way you are running your company today work in this brave new world? Is some form of the 5% Rule your most hopeful way forward?

6

Front-Loading Negotiations

Know What You Want Going In

As I hope you have come to see, the embodiment of Lean economic management is the 5% Rule. In this chapter, we will look at how the 5% Rule applies to corporate acquisitions, which happen often in the high-tech world. Later, we will look at how the Rule can be used for most consequential decisions throughout a company.

Stepping In

As you might have guessed that last 5% is not a rock-solid number—indeed, it may be just 1%, or as much as

6% or 7%, depending on the conclusion of an acquisition, which can be brief or protracted.

What is crucial is that the first 5% remain just that: 5%.

When does my role as CEO begin? In my experience, during an acquisition there is no need for me to get involved until the ground has been prepared by our corporate development team. There are two reasons for that. First, the team knows what they are doing, and I trust their ability to winnow out deals which could be synergistic to our business. But just as important, I do not want to waste my time getting involved prematurely.

Like many other high-tech firms of our size, our company is contacted monthly, and sometimes weekly, by companies hoping to be acquired. We will pass on most of them. So, if I were to get involved with each of them from the initial contact, I would be wasting a sizable fraction of my work week—and the equivalent of a generous sum of money and bandwidth—on fruitless distractions.

But sometimes, the corporate development team will come to me and say, "You know, we should look at this company." In many companies, at this point even more people in the organization will get involved.

But we have learned from experience to take a different path. For us, this is when my 5% timeline begins.

As CEO, when our corporate development team says a company is worth looking at, I am the first person involved, before any formal discussion or due diligence starts.

This first 5% is much more important in this discussion than the last 5%, the latter being pretty much pro forma, dealing with final terms, board approval, and closing matters. By contrast, there is truly little that is predictable about the first 5%.

A Question of Price

We begin by asking a lot of tough questions. One is price. Will the deal even be in the ballpark? If the number the other company wants is the one we are willing to pay, great; negotiations are over. But as you might imagine, that does not happen very often.

The more likely scenario is that there is a difference, large or small, between what they want and what we are willing to pay. So, high-level, informal negotiations begin. Now it is incumbent on me to make some important decisions—in particular, what we are willing to bid.

As CEO, this is not only my job, but also a fiduciary responsibility. Once I have produced a bid, I must see how the other side reacts. Until each of us has stated what we believe the value of the transaction to be, nothing more can happen. And if the other company wants to be coy and not state a value, then it is on me to tell them what the deal is worth.

On this last issue, it may surprise you to learn just how many companies enter one of these negotiations wanting to be acquired but having no idea the price they want. That's because they are hoping they will get lucky and get offered an amount beyond their wildest hopes. Or they are afraid they are asking too little and will leave a fortune on the table. Or they have a high valuation in mind, and they are afraid of insulting us, and that we will not even counter.

Of the seven acquisitions that NetScout has undertaken in the last few years, five companies had no clear idea how much they wanted. Tellingly, the two companies that did know were large enterprises. In fact, they were larger than us. The five that did not know were much smaller. This suggests that the smaller, younger companies simply did not have the expertise or experience to undertake the necessary self-audit; the big companies did.

Some smaller companies—say, with revenues less than $100 million—will begin negotiations by saying, "Well, you know, we have invested so much in this. We have so many people. Oh, and we have five other companies interested in us. We have 20 customers. Do not look at our revenue for last year, as we are expecting big growth in the coming year." They will do everything except say what the price should be. And frankly, at that moment I do not care about any of those other things. I only want the ballpark price range, because that will determine if the conversation continues: Should we spend the rest of our time on this deal, or should we walk away? We want to know what they really think they are worth. If they are thinking $100 million, and we are thinking $10 million, why are we even talking?

Truthfully, if I were in a comparable situation 20 years ago, and you had asked me what my company was worth, I would not have been able to answer that question either. It is an extremely hard evaluation unless you are an experienced company executive or a venture capitalist.

What I have found most often skews that evaluation by the other party is that they work backwards from the amount of return they want. They start with, "We spent

$100 million, so now are worth $300 million," rather than looking at their true market value for a potential acquirer.

For our part, determining that value is its own challenge. It is one reason we do not go outside our turf in making acquisitions. Having extensive domain knowledge is critical to success. That is yet another reason you need to get involved in the first 5% of the process—not just because you may be the CEO, but because you may have worked in this industry as long as anyone in your company.

Assuming we agree on a potential price, the table quickly turns. Now it is our move. We do a marketing job, telling our counterparts about our history, our culture, our businesses—even though we have not yet decided to buy them. Why? Because now there is a possibility that we may make the acquisition, and we want to foreclose our counterpart considering any other potential suitors. In fact, I typically spend much of my initial 5% doing more selling than negotiating.

Once the general guidelines have been established, I leave the final negotiating to the team, returning only when we need to close.

Give Them a Number

Once you get past the matter of earn-outs, negotiations come down to one question: "How much money do you want?"

Nobody ever really answers that question with a number. They are likely to reply with some version of "as much as possible." They want the acquirer to name a number first. So, I give them one, because if they cannot produce a well-thought-out number, then they are going to have to start with mine. This is not a negotiating tactic; it is a way of feeling out the other party. Are they serious? Are their expectations realistic? How much money do they really want? In Chapter 12, "Don't Worry About Leaving Money on the Table," I further expand on our negotiating style and associated rationale.

Asking the Right Questions

Once we have determined that the likely deal price is within our predicted range, then the next question I ask is whether there is a good cultural fit between the leadership of our company and theirs—another aspect of the initial 5% effort.

This is not a question I verbalize, but rather one I ask myself, and I listen to my intuition for an answer. After my many years in business, one can feel if a merger is going to succeed, especially when you are trying to acquire someone in your market space. If I get a bad feeling, based on gut and deep experience, that's reason enough to walk away from the deal.

If a company passes the cultural match test, I inquire into their motives for selling. Not only "Why are you selling?" but "Why are you selling to us?" Are we their first or best option?

Obviously, to the last question they are going to say we are their first choice. So, I dig deeper, following that up with "Why are we your first choice?" The answer is usually illuminating. For example, some founders say they have always wanted to be part of a bigger technology company. Others are obviously just exhausted; they have taken the company as far as they can, and now they just want to hand it off to someone else for the next phase. (Of course, they will rarely admit that.)

In answer to the question, "Why us?" some companies will try to force our hand, by claiming they are talking to other companies. To this we immediately respond, "Sorry, but we are not interested in entering into an auction." We encourage them to pursue other opportunities, and if they all fall through, then come back to us, and we will reconsider.

This either ends the negotiation, or—and this may surprise some readers, given that deals like this must be based on mutual trust—they admit, without saying so, that there are no other better candidates. That does not kill the deal, but that broken trust makes the probability of a successful resolution much smaller.

Ultimately when we ask these questions about why the company wants to sell and why they want to sell to us, we are less interested in their answers than we are in their thought processes. Many companies we negotiate with answer similarly: "We want to grow faster, and we have two strategic options: either grow into a bigger company by selling to a bigger company or go public. We are exploring both options."

We do not put much weight on these answers, but the questions are important because they open a pathway to a deeper dialog, one that enables us to get a feel for the personalities of the players on the other side and the nature of the assets we may be buying.

Trust and Transparency

It may surprise readers to learn that we typically conduct a substantial portion of this initial discussion with quite simple and generic nondisclosure agreements (NDAs). A complicated NDA requires the legal teams from both sides to get involved, and invariably they get caught up in multiple iterations before finalizing the NDA. Using a generic NDA in the initial phase of acquisition conversations cuts down the paperwork and time investment.

Instead, we build everything on trust and transparency, which creates velocity. Early in the 5% Rule time frame and sometimes even during the first meeting, I can see into the inner workings of the other company. I can determine whether our investors and board will like a deal or not. And, when it is the case, I can see why the other company is losing money despite having a good team and technology.

Without this transparency and trust, while I am waiting for the NDAs to be approved by all parties, all I can do is look at basic financial metrics, and they are never enough. Instead, with the time we would have wasted not trusting each other, we can get started on our dialog and the deal.

During this dialog, we make some interesting discoveries and come to some definitive conclusions. Sometimes I find myself saying, "Oh, this is a really good company." When that happens, we immediately shift into the mode of selling our company as a wonderful place to work.

As noted, the goal then becomes foreclosing any other opportunities in the eyes of the other company. And that shift, when it happens, usually consumes much of the rest of my initial 5% commitment.

Meet and Greet

A whole lot happens during that first 5% interval. For example, I meet with the company's top executives at least once or twice. Sometimes, if things are going well, these meetings will last all day and typically finish with dinner, which is a wonderful way to learn about each other in a casual space. It is important to note that we almost never go to the other company for meetings, until the formal due diligence is almost done. They come to us.

After those initial meetings and dinner, I usually remove myself from the negotiation process. I have done my part. By this point we know what the deal is likely to be, we have learned about the other company, and we have plumbed the personalities and motivations of its founders and top executives.

Most of all, we have decided that this potential acquisition is worth the effort. It is time for me to get out of the picture and let the professionals on our development team take over.

Now, you may ask, what if the other company is lying to us? What if they take advantage of this trust, misrepresenting their value and assets to get past the first cut? The answer lies in our initial selection process: We look only at companies either in our domain space or in an adjacent market. We do not buy companies just for revenue.

This means we typically already know the company, or at least we know everything about its market. That is an especially important requirement for agreeing to meet with the other company in the first place. Our philosophy is never to buy a company we do not know in a market we do not understand.

As a result, lying or hiding details is just not that easy. I will ask a prospect, "Who are your competitors?" If the list they come back with is different than our own knowledge of the market, I will then ask, "Why don't you consider ABC company a competitor?"

Some companies will try to get away with the clichéd argument that, "Really, nobody does what we do." I always reply, "How is that possible? What are you doing differently? Why isn't your business interesting enough to attract competitors?" They are not going to win through obfuscation, because we have the facts and the numbers. Eventually they will have to back up their claims with similar facts and numbers.

Most of my first 5% participation rests on an intuition that this is a quality deal, but it is only that: a gut feeling. After the initial 5%, that subjective sense is confirmed with empirical data.

The 90%

If a deal survives the first 5%, it is time to confirm my subjective sense. This means not only handing off the project to others but also continuously increasing the number of participants from our company in due diligence.

Typically, we begin with 4 or 5 people; but soon thereafter it may climb to as many as 10. By the time we are done, there may be 20 of us working on the deal, including outside advisors, depending on the size and complexity of the business we are hoping to acquire.

What are all these people doing? All the due diligence required to ensure the company is both a good fit for NetScout and worth what we are paying for it. This means inviting the other company to make a product presentation to our marketing and salespeople, a technology presentation to our R&D people, and other such exercises, like creating a formal "data room." This is also when we may visit the other company and scrutinize its facilities and equipment. Depending on the size of the deal, it can be a very lengthy and detailed process, and deservedly so. The last thing we want is to get drawn in by oversized claims about a company's product line or capabilities, and overpay for an acquisition.

Even as the number of our people involved grows, and even as the deal gets closer to certainty, the number of people who know about it here at NetScout remains exceedingly small, usually little more than the number who are part of the due diligence. We want our employees focused on doing their jobs well, not distracted by a deal that may never actually happen. If they start running scenarios through their heads about life at NetScout after the potential merger, and then it falls through, we have wasted their time and done them a disservice.

Simply put, what happens in this 90% is what every company does during an acquisition. And although we are particularly good at due diligence, I do not claim that we are that much better than most other companies, especially those that do a lot of mergers and acquisitions.

No, the real difference lies in that first 5%. That part—my part—if done right, enables us to get right down to business, or kill the deal, at the very start.

The Risks of Skipping the First 5%

In most companies, the CEO does not get involved at the start but allows the corporate development team to run the process until it is time for a final decision on the acquisition. Only then, halfway, or even two-thirds of the way through negotiations, is the CEO brought in, briefed, and asked to decide whether the deal should proceed.

In theory, this seems like a sound strategy. Why waste the CEO's valuable time on a deal before it looks to be successful? But in practice, this strategy is fraught with potential downfalls.

The biggest risk is human nature. A development team, having worked months on a deal, is likely to become psychologically committed to making it happen, if only to justify their personal investment. Instead of being advocates for their company's long-term success, they may, often unconsciously, become advocates for the successful completion of the deal. Understandably, they fall in love with the deal. At best, they are committed to helping the company through a good acquisition. But more often, subconsciously they end up working against the good of their own company, because they are more concerned with getting the CEO to sign on to the acquisition. It is far better for the CEO to get involved at the very beginning and make the go or no-go decision as early as possible, before the development team becomes overly invested, sparing everyone the potential grief.

Final 5%

If the first 5% involves the use of my personal business and people skills, the final 5%—in which I once again get involved in the negotiations—requires me to leverage my power as CEO. Again, like the preceding 90%, this part of the process is not much different than it is for other companies acquiring.

Say that the other company looks worthy, the fit looks good, and we are near an acceptable purchase price. At that point, my team and I made a transition to talking about our company, why joining us will be such a good deal for them, why we are a special company.

For my part, I will talk about our focus on retaining talent from our acquisitions, how we mix organizational levels to ensure that new employees coming over from the acquisition quickly settle into a new and worthy role at NetScout. I describe our plans for revenue growth, our stock options (restricted stock units), the trust we place in our employees, and a score of other factors that make NetScout a special place to work and grow.

Our goal? We want them to fall in love with NetScout. That way, if the deal goes through, transitioning their employees to our culture will happen more swiftly and smoothly. Just as important, we want to create a barrier, in case some other company gets wind of the deal and tries to sweep in at the last moment. If we have done our job right, the company we wish to acquire will see the advantages of being part of NetScout as being so valuable that its management may not even look at a bid less than twice what we are offering.

That is the beginning of the final 5%. The rest, at least for me, is standard merger and acquisitions stuff: nailing down a purchase price, then getting approval for the deal from the board of directors and NetScout shareholders. Because I was involved in the process at the very beginning and at the very end, I do not go into these presentations and votes with only a limited amount of briefing beforehand. Instead, I can speak from a place of experience and authority.

In the end, we know the company we have acquired—its strengths and weaknesses, its key employees, and its culture. After the ink on the deal has dried, we are well prepared for the next phase—the merging of the two enterprises, which is the subject of the Chapter 7.

CHAPTER

7

Why Earn-Outs Are Bad for Acquisitions
Make a Clean Break

Everyone loves earn-outs. These contractual agreements, made between parties in an acquisition, enable pay-outs to continue to sellers, usually as a percentage of gross sales or earnings, for years after an actual sale is consummated. Sellers love them because, with luck, earn-outs can get them the total price they wanted, instead of the price they got.

Buyers love earn-outs because they offer a form of insurance: They can make the acquisition at a discount price, and they will not have to pay the full price unless the acquired company's performance lives up to expectations. The same holds true for the shareholders of both companies.

As you may expect, given what you have read so far, at NetScout we have a different view of earn-outs. We do not like them. I do not say this as in, "It's a gray area for us." I mean we think earn-outs are dangerous to the future of the newly combined enterprise.

There are several reasons why we believe this: First, the creation of earn-outs is predicated on bad faith. The assumption is that, as the buyer, we cannot trust the assets we are acquiring. What are those assets? They include technology, products, and customers, but most of all, they are people—the employees of the acquired company.

Inserting an earn-out into a deal says the buyer does not trust these employees and, worse, the employees are going to be put to a performance test after the acquisition before they receive more money. That is why we consider this instrument a nonstarter: If we really do not trust the employees of the company to be acquired, then we should not be acquiring that company. In doing so we would be entering a deal from a compromised position.

Second, in adding an earn-out, we would admit that we have not done our homework, particularly that I have not done my 5%. The willingness to enter into such an open-ended agreement suggests that we might be buying either the wrong company or that we do not know enough about it to make an informed offer. We do not have the time, energy, or inclination to perform our due diligence, to be confident enough in the deal not to include an earn-out—and if that is the case, should we really be making the deal?

Third, if we really do think we are making the right deal, then why wouldn't we do the work to produce a defensible and complete offer? Anything short of that—especially offering an earn-out—suggests a conflict between wanting to acquire that company and not really understanding or trusting its viability. That conflict should have already been resolved in the 5% process.

Finally, earn-outs create, in a newly merged company, two groups with competing goals, thus making them de facto competitors. One group, the original acquirers, will work toward the long-term success of the new company; the other group, the acquired, will work toward the short-term success of the earn-out deal. If the overall company is not going to hit its numbers, the acquired portion will still fight—even at the expense of the overall enterprise—to show that it has met its earn-out goals.

This could tear the newly merged company in two. Under these circumstances, the two organizations cannot integrate quickly, nor can the product lines integrate—because if they do, how can the acquired company measure whether it is hitting its earn-out targets? How will the acquired company know if its people have payday coming or if they will stay after the payday? From the start, the new company begins pulling itself in opposite directions. There is no great argument for applying the 5% Rule.

These opposing management interests force all kinds of unnatural decisions on a new company. For example, leadership will find themselves making crucial business decisions based on limited information because they have not made the necessary measurements. Leadership will operate under two sets of rules regarding the employees. Further, leadership will find itself creating two sets of corporate goals, which will prove especially dangerous if those goals are in any way anti-thetical. But even if they are not, divided attention and resources may mean a failure to achieve either goal.

Moreover, almost by definition, if a company is running successfully, then it will be almost impossible to measure whether it will meet the earn-out goals because the operations of the acquired company will be—properly—too intermingled with those of the acquiring company to differentiate.

A company divided against itself, suffering endemic mistrust among its employees, and confused about its goals, is not the kind of place where talented, ambitious people will want to work. Thus, it is not unusual for earn-out-defined mergers to quickly experience a loss of key talent.

The Value of Predictability

One company with which we have had close dealings has made several acquisitions, most of them featuring earn-outs. All have ended badly, some even resulting in lawsuits, expensive financial settlements, and irreparably broken relationships amongst the founders.

By comparison, NetScout has purchased more than 10 companies over its history. None have experienced this kind of fallout because none of our deals were dependent on some elusive and unpredictable future performance. On the contrary, during my 5% I consciously have eschewed future earn-outs and have operated in the present. That is, we have determined an acceptable price for each of these companies, negotiated a deal, and from the moment each deal was signed, we have strived to operate as a unified company with common goals, reward systems, rules, and culture.

Once again, this strategy is congruent with the goal to simplify and streamline the process: we pay in the present rather than offering probable future earn-outs, we treat everyone fairly, and we get on with business.

At one point, people have told me, "You are trying to buy this company on the West Coast. Your approach just will not work in Silicon Valley. They demand earn-outs there." But our acquisition strategy succeeded on the West Coast, just as it has on the East Coast, in Europe, and in Asia, without earn-outs.

Faking Yourself Out

A word of warning to those who are not yet ready to jettison earn-outs in their entirety: Pseudo-earn-outs can be just as divisive and destructive.

If a company has many divisions, each with its own bonus plan based on its independent business objectives, this is not an earn-out. But it is its philosophical cousin. It demands different measurement programs and offers different rewards for performance in what should be a single corporate effort.

Despite having multiple business units, NetScout has instituted a common bonus plan. It consists of a total bonus accrual based on the top line (and other metrics) of the combined company, but with the bonus distribution partially weighted toward business unit performance. This means that if the top goals do not work, everyone is affected. Happily, that dark scenario has occurred rarely. What happens most often is that everyone gets a bigger bonus at the end of the year because they were all marching in the same direction, as a single team, with a common purpose.

The bottom line is that there are no exceptions to our no-earn-out philosophy. In fact, the people most likely to refuse a no-earn-out deal are the people whose companies you do not want to acquire anyway. They will argue that they are the special case in which a no-earn-out deal will succeed, but that is simply not true. In our experience with diverse acquisitions, no matter the size, location, or profitability of these firms, our approach has proven to be applicable universally.

Praying for Failure

In the end, earn-outs make no one happy. They may seem to benefit from the leadership of an acquired company, who, if they hit some performance targets, could make more money than they would have with a fixed deal. But ironically, those same individuals, if given an earn-out, will inevitably complain later that they got the worst end of the deal.

Why? Because once the deal is signed, the perspective of the acquired company changes. The acquirer presents the earn-out as a reward: "I'll be paying you $20 million more than the $30 million I could have paid." But the acquired company thinks: "If we are worth $50 million and we are getting only $30 million now, then we are being penalized by $20 million. I should have gotten the whole amount on day one."

On the flip side, I have observed earn-out deals in which people in the C-suite of the acquiring company are almost wishing their counterparts in the acquired company do not make their targets so they do not have to be paid the earn-out money. Sometimes, in a self-fulfilling prophecy, they even withhold investing in the acquired company so it cannot reach its earn-out targets. How self-destructive is that? How can the newly combined company ever succeed with that kind of attitude at the top?

Working Toward Mutual Success

Now let us look at the alternative scenario, the one without the burden of an earn-out.

Let us take our $30 million upfront deal with the $20 million earn-out. What does that really mean? It means that the $30 million was too low for the acquired firm to accept. But it also means that the $50 million is a pipe dream, a number the acquiring company pulled out of thin air because it does not believe the other company will ever meet its numbers.

Indeed, as we have just discussed, the acquiring company may even impede—actively or passively—the acquired company's progress toward that goal.

So, in the end, one side thinks, "What is the problem? I am giving them a bonus." And the other side is thinking, "I'm getting punished for agreeing to a discount on my real worth." How can these two parties ever reconcile and work together? They are always going to be resentful. Yet if you look around at the business world, you see this failed merger model playing out hundreds of times every year.

Instead, why not compromise? Meet halfway. At, say, a $35 million to $40 million fixed price, the acquirer would be making a realistic offer while eliminating the risk of the acquired company fulfilling its earn-out deal. At the same time, the acquired company is getting a fair price, without the risk of falling short of the earn-out's terms. That is fairness in action—and it usually is the centerpiece of the 5% portion of the negotiation: deciding not what you want, but what will be perceived as fair by both parties.

With an agreed-on, fixed price, the deal can be consummated with both parties aligned in pursuit of common goals. On day one, because the new company is not dealing with two different goals, you can integrate the regions, cultures, product lines, and organizations of the two businesses. Then day two—and all those that follow—will look like a continuation of day one, because everyone is marching in alignment, not pulling in different directions. There is nothing more important for your company's ultimate success.

In fact, I can all but guarantee that if you abandon the earn-out as a tool of acquisition, the companies you acquire—or those that acquire you—will do better than they would have with an earn-out. And that is the biggest bonus of all.

8

Be a Problem-Solver, Not a Solution Provider

Give Them What They Need, Not What They Ask For

About 30 years ago, I learned one of the most valuable lessons of my professional life, which became an essential component of Lean decision-making. Here is how it happened.

As young entrepreneurs in our early 30s, my cofounder and I walked into a meeting with a vice president of a then-mighty computer company in the Boston area. We were there to sell our products and services, and we were confident to the point of being cocky. In fact, we were so excited about our message that as soon as we finished the introductions, we launched into a pitch about the products we had to offer, why we were better than any of our competitors, how we had the industry's best engineering team, and how we alone could provide the solutions that customers needed.

The VP, who was much older and more experienced than we were, listened without comment for 15 minutes, and we thought we were making a favorable impression. Then, finally, he put a hand up to silence us and said to me, "Son, I know you are excited and very capable, but have I even told you what my problem is? Or whether we even need your product? This meeting is now over. I advise both of you, for your next meeting, do not start selling what you have until your potential customer has explained the problem that needs to be solved."

We left with some embarrassment but also with some valuable advice. Silently, I still thank that executive for the lesson.

Problems Before Solutions

To me, one of the most dangerous phrases in modern business is when a company announces that it is in the "solutions" business. If that phrase remains only a cliché, a buzzword, then the company is safe. But once a company starts operating as a solutions-oriented business, it may be headed for trouble.

This may sound counterintuitive. Who does not want to provide solutions to their customers? That is how embedded this term has become in daily business language. Let me explain: The problem with a solution orientation is that it bypasses a particularly crucial step. It starts out, properly, shifting the company's attention toward the customer's needs. But it quickly devolves into a procedural shortcut, moving past the customer's actual, real, pain-producing problem, to focus instead on the "solution" for a problem the company has, unilaterally, decided on.

This equation is wrong on both ends. First, until you can characterize a problem, you cannot really come up with a viable solution. Second, given the nature of technological innovation, customers may not actually know the best solution available to them, even though they may describe their requirements in terms of the solution they want to implement. The result, often, is a compromised effort by everyone involved.

The Problem with Problems

People do not like problems. Problems burn up energy, waste time, and increase the risk of failure. So, it is natural for both employees and managers—especially the smartest and most aggressive ones—to glance at a problem, assume they understand it, and then rush off to implement their response. Responding quickly is emotionally rewarding; you feel like you are doing something positive, that you are ameliorating the situation, that you are being a hero both to your company and to the customer. You are implementing the fix, and companies reward people who do that. In other words, all the incentives are there for your people to skip that messy problem stuff and work on a response.

Described this way, the danger becomes obvious. If you do not understand the problem, the odds are high that you will not come up with the best solution. Indeed, given the dangers of a precipitous response—not least that you will lose time and money (and potentially the customer) if you must backtrack and start over—you might be better off doing nothing than doing something.

There is no better reason for adopting the deliberative front-end approach of the 5% Rule.

A solutions-focused company creates a customizable solution applicable for the general marketplace. Rather than fully understanding the nuances of a customer's unique problem, it looks for ways to make its existing solution fit the problem. A problem-solving company or individual, however, will take the time to redefine, reduce, and fine-tune the problem before it ever attempts to solve that problem. That is, it will use the initial 5% of its approach to determine the real need.

But even that is not enough. Here again, there is a danger of oversimplification. We tend to think that all problems are reducible. But not all problems can be simplified, or often they cannot be simplified as much as we think they can. Furthermore, some problems are worth solving, and some are just so intractable that the only solution is either to ignore them or simply to pay to make them go away.

So, how do you effectively assess a problem? We will look at that next.

A Real-Life Example

Most negotiation classes teach future negotiators to develop and use the best alternative to a negotiated agreement (BATNA) framework to guide their negotiation. BATNA is intended to represent the most advantageous alternative that a negotiating party can take if an agreement cannot be made and negotiations fail. The process of formulating a BATNA involves listing all alternatives, considering the pros and cons, the costs, and benefits of each, and how those align with your interests and goals. However, as taught, a critical first step is missing from the BATNA framework: a clear understanding of the problem you are trying to solve with the negotiation.

We had a seasoned contract attorney who joined our legal team several years ago. Early in her tenure with NetScout, she was involved in a negotiation that reached an impasse. As this negotiation was for the creation of a highly strategic business partnership, I was brought in to be briefed on the outstanding issues. After being presented with the list of what the team had classified as "open," I asked her what the one obligation was the other side was seeking to impose that she saw as being the most challenging to overcome. The attorney looked surprised and confused.

"You are forgetting the bigger problem we are trying to solve," I told her, "which is how the parties can do business together." We then talked through what she thought was the "biggest" open issue and identified some of our existing business processes that could act as systematic controls for managing the obligations associated with this issue should it be triggered. I then directed her to go back to the negotiation table and only concede on this one point.

The agreement was signed with only the one concession given and the rest of the open issues dropped.

First Question: Why?

How do you effectively address a problem? Experience has taught me that always the key is to focus on the why? first instead of on the what? or even the how?

In problem-solving, we tend to emphasize what the problem is and then attack those symptoms. Secondarily, we attend to how the problem occurred, and then we try to fix the underlying processes. In the short-term, both approaches usually provide satisfying solutions. We see that everything is working again, and we walk away patting our backs at what clever detectives we are. And then, six months later, the problem appears again.

However, if we move upstream from the what? and how? and we focus on why? the problem occurred, we are often surprised to discover a root cause, or a systemic issue, or a missed opportunity that seems benign but through a series of causal events, bursts out later as our problem. It's like curing a case of bronchitis, only to have it recur every few months, never noticing the patient is a heavy smoker. That patient looks better every time we implement a solution. Nevertheless, the patient is heading toward a much worse, and less fixable, problem.

So, that is the first half of our new equation: Take the time to fully understand the problem; then simplify the problem by searching for the why?

Finding a Solution

Now for the second half: the solution. Here, too, there is truth hidden behind the obvious. That is, even if we do not jump to conclusions, but carefully and systematically understand the problem and then execute on the apparent, initial, solution, we can still miss the mark. Why? Because it is rare that we can impose our solution on a customer. In fact, that is one of the inherent dangers of being a "solution provider": implicit in that philosophy is that the customer plays the defining role in determining what that solution should be.

But the reality is, in our fast-moving world, customers are always better editors than they are authors. Too often they only know what they like (or do not like) when they see it, and not before.

How can you expect it to be any different? If your product or service is as state-of-the-art as it should be, then your customer has never seen anything like it before. Place yourself in the final months of 2001: Apple Computer, as it was then known, was calling on retailers to determine what new product they wanted to see from the company. How many of those queried, do you think, replied, "We think our customers will want a small, rechargeable device about the size of a deck of cards, with an internal hard disk drive and a tiny LCD screen and a revolutionary navigational wheel. And it should be able to download and save several hundred of those new-fangled MP3 music files. Oh, and price it at less than $400"?

None. The announcement of the original Apple iPod hit like a bombshell. Other than a few design engineers who predicted it, nobody saw it coming. MP3 recording was something done by college kids, many of whom may have been breaking the law by illegal downloading. The iPod, with the company's iTunes music downloading service, rationalized what was, until that moment, a splintering digital music industry.

If Apple had limited itself to delivering to its Macintosh users only the solution they wanted, it would have settled for a more powerful, cheaper Mac, forever. The company did deliver that, but it also delivered another product consumers never asked for, and it followed that with a string of other unrequested, nonsolutions, notably the iPhone and iPad. To date, Apple has sold 400 million iPods. Add to that more than one billion iPhones, and 300 million iPads. Apple has changed the world of consumer electronics, created three new product categories worth a total of a trillion dollars, and made Apple Inc. the most valuable manufacturing company in history.

Why? Because Steve Jobs did not ask customers for solutions, but instead set out to identify their problems: chaos in the digital music industry, the proliferation of too many portable devices, too much wasted capability (and thus cost) in laptop computers. Once he identified these pain points, he could create true solutions, to which those customers could make only the tiniest contributions beforehand.

This focus on solving real problems, and relieving real pain, has been the propellant of many successful companies. Two billion people in the world had no idea they wanted to be part of a social network until Facebook showed it to them. Everyone assumed that the only way to get rid of the junk in their attic or garage was to either donate it or hold a garage sale, until eBay showed them differently. Engineers did not know they needed a pocket scientific calculator until HP announced the Model 35.

That said, once customers and consumers began to assimilate these inventions or innovative new services into their professional and private lives, they could offer all kinds of recommendations for improvements. As I said, consumers are brilliant editors, usually better than the creators of these inventions, but the solutions themselves must be written by your team.

But if you reserve problem-solving in new or enhanced product development for yourself, and not your customer, how do you know when to stop? If those customers cannot really tell you what they want, why not give them everything? Just cover all the possible bases by adding one feature after another. Then let your customers edit out anything they do not want. Obviously, this is not cost-effective, for one. Plus, it leaves the product development process open-ended, and endless. Worse, it leads to excess—the smarter your engineers are, the more unnecessary features they can produce, at an ever-faster pace.

Here is where the 5% Rule can help. If you believe from the start, as we do, that customers are good editors, then you do not build your new product introduction model on the premise that customers are only given a fait accompli solution. Rather, you create a development cycle and go to market strategy that purposely takes into consideration the use of customers not just as a governor on potentially overengineered solutions but also as your most vocal salesperson. What do I mean by that? Using your customer as editors means that you will have to educate them along the way, so they remain supportive of your efforts, rather than an impediment. In the process, if you can convince them of the value of your efforts, then selling them to the value of a result will also be a whole lot easier.

So, back to our question: If you are reserving initial product development for yourself, how do you know when to put on the brakes? The answer, I believe, as many others in the industry do, is that you must begin with the most stripped-down version—the *minimal viable product*, as it is called—of your new offering. Then you must challenge every feature you want to add to it.

Further, that challenge process should be negative in its orientation. That is, for every new feature proposed, the challenge should be to explain why it is not needed. Even further, if that feature passes this first hurdle, the debate should shift to whether implementing a mediocre version—that is, a feature that sounds good on paper but does not fulfill its potential—would be an improvement over not having that feature at all. Only then, if you can show it is necessary and that it will be a superior implementation, should this feature be added to the final design.

Finally, let me share with you a practical solution based on real-life experience. You must learn to say "stop!" to your most talented engineers. This is the only practical way to manage complexity. Software engineers, given the chance, will devote 99% of their time to writing code. Like most people, they emphasize what they do best, what they were hired for. That is what they want. What you—and by extension, your company, your customers, and your shareholders—should want is for these engineers to spend the last 50% of their time coding (doing), and the first 50% understanding the problem, and then taking out complexity (thinking). As part of this exercise, the initial design should be done without addressing specific use cases and with truly little domain knowledge.

How do you enforce that new ratio—especially when it plays against the natural tendencies of those programmers? The usual way: by rewarding the proper behavior. Recognize and honor elegant, simple, and appropriate solutions, and enjoy the powerful result. Then let your customer's domain knowledge, and specific use cases, perfect it.

In summary:

- Do not try solving a problem before all the players have agreed on what the problem is: It is much easier to draw consensus on the problem rather than the solution. You can accelerate this agreement process by simplifying the problem.

- Agree on the why? first, not the what? If you cannot agree on why you are doing something, there is no point in going forward.

- Always elucidate a concise summary of the problem you are trying to solve. Get agreement on a crisp articulation of the problem before starting any work.

- Keep the goal in mind: Who is the audience? What are we trying to achieve?

9

Control the Timetable of Disruptions

Choose Your Fate

Your business is going to be disrupted. You can count on it. And right about the time you finally recover from that disruption, you will be disrupted again. So why not take control over your destiny and disrupt yourself?

You can control the timeline of disruption and, in fact, may want to accelerate it when disruption appears imminent. This is the very definition of what applying the 5% Rule can help you do: Provide the company with the guardrails it needs to see and shape its own fate.

Change is the one reality common to all modern businesses. At the center of the global economy are two primary forces: Moore's law and Metcalfe's law.

The first, which is better known, says that the power of computer chips doubles every couple (these days, three or four) of years. And because those chips can now be found, by the billions, in every aspect of modern life, about every business is destined to get revised—or more likely, turned upside down—every few years.

Today's winners are tomorrow's losers, and vice versa, and what your business will look like in a few years will bear little resemblance to what it looks like today. You may have read that Moore's law is "slowing," but slowing is a relative term. This principle has defined the modern business world for 50 years now and will for decades more. So far, no contemporary company has bet successfully against Moore's law.

Metcalfe's law is a little more obscure, but it is just as influential. It says that networks increase in value with every new node or user on that network. The magnitude of this increase has long been a subject of debate, but it is agreed to be a multiple of each added user. The ultimate example of this law is, of course, the internet.

Moore's law not only guarantees continuous change but also it affects every company that enters the digital world. Metcalfe's law, similarly, rewards connectivity and networking. Combine both forces and you can see why disruption is not only inevitable but pervasive. No matter what industry you are in—even the most traditional—it can and will be virtualized. Once a company steps aboard the bullet train created by these laws, that disruption will happen periodically, and its impact will be both devastating and transformative to the status quo.

There is no product, business, industry, or sector that is immune to this effect. Further, these disruptions will not come just from predictable directions, like your direct competitors or even competitors in adjacent industries. They will come from companies in industries that, until now, had nothing to do with you.

Think of the iPhone, introduced by a company known for making personal computers, and how it upended the global cellular phone industry. Or how desktop publishing software shuttered thousands of small print shops. Or how mapmakers were disrupted by GPS. Or classified ads by eBay and Craigslist. And these days, look at the chaos being created by the arrival of artificial intelligence. A company in an industrial sector and from a part of the world that you have never even considered a competitor can arise without warning, leaving your company little time to produce a strategy to survive.

We know all this. We know disruption is coming. We even have an innovative idea when it is coming, especially if we are vigilant and leaders in our industries. So why wait around for the next disruption to hit? Why not go on the offensive: Do not fight it; rather, proactively disrupt yourself.

One way to look at this is that you must occasionally endure short-term pain for long-term gain. But I prefer to put a positive spin on the process. Think of self-disruption as a form of innovation—not just of your products or service, but of your approach to your business. Disruption may indeed mean revamping your offerings, but it can also mean changing your business model, or your supply and distribution chains, or your targeted customers.

Some companies, anticipating the next great disruption, may move to abandon their hardware business and move down-market to applications or software platform solutions. That is what IBM did, selling off its legendary computer business and shifting into enterprise solutions. Other companies may want to strip away less-profitable businesses and focus on narrower but more profitable enterprises—or just the opposite. Internally, you may want to reorganize your company, instituting a new communications and reporting apparatus, or changing your salary, bonus, and stock plans. Externally, you may look for new acquisitions, or bring a contract salesforce in-house, or just the opposite. Or you'll choose to circumvent your network of retailers and offer your products directly online.

In other words, for your company to remain viable and vital, you should consider everything to be on the table for change.

An Industry Turned Upside Down

Let me tell you the story of the most memorable disruption in NetScout's history. In 1991, the young NetScout decided to build proprietary hardware for our monitoring solution. Why? Because in those days, companies in our industry were judged by the quality not just of their hardware but of the components of that hardware. The problem was that, although our company knew how to design hardware, we really did not know how to manufacture hardware cost-effectively, at least not well. In addition, we wanted to build hardware because we saw no other viable option available in the market. We had convinced ourselves that our type of specialized hardware design was the only way to go, and we believed it was a quick way to differentiate ourselves and make money.

Well, we got all the way to early field trials of our new hardware. We wrote a complete business plan supporting the brilliance of our idea, emphasizing the uniqueness and performance of our associated solution. We went out looking for venture capital money to support our new initiative.

We even convinced and hired three executives, giving them a lot of stock in the company, to run our finance, sales, and marketing operations, based on this business plan. They were as excited by the opportunity as we, the two founders, were.

In hindsight, I am thankful we never secured the VC (venture capital) funding. Because soon afterwards, AMD and Intel settled their old lawsuit over sourcing of the microprocessor. Suddenly, a complete motherboard, with an embedded Intel chip (i386 at that time) became as powerful as the custom chips we were using on our intelligent hardware accelerator, yet at a fraction of the cost. This turned our product assumptions and business plan upside down, and suddenly, over the course of a weekend, we were at risk of losing our executive team.

By this point, we had spent close to $1 million of NetScout's money and all the life savings of the two cofounders—a huge commitment at that early stage. We had announced, publicly, our commitment to the custom hardware strategy. Now we had to tell the world—not least our few existing customers—that we were completely changing our game plan and strategic direction.

We had the option of modifying our hardware design and limping along for some time, before going in a completely new direction, based on off-the-shelf hardware. But we also knew that full disruption was just around the corner, and we decided to accelerate it, instead of fighting it.

This was the hardest decision we had ever made. Happily, we managed to keep the executive team together, despite us getting out of the hardware business and moving to a software-centric strategy. In fact, these executives stayed with us for a decade after that, until they retired.

From this pivotal moment, we swore we would never let our company leap into a new business just because it was exciting or because others in our industry were doing the same, without doing our due diligence ahead of time—the 5% Rule. Just as important, we learned the value of controlling the timetable of disruption.

Telling the full story of NetScout's first 30 years would talk volumes. But it can also be told simply as the story of three disruptions: We began as a company whose primary source of revenue was through the sale of purpose-built network monitoring hardware devices. It proved to be a very profitable business; as networks grew, so too did the need for our devices, and hardware has a natural refresh cycle forcing customers to come back to us every three to four years to get updated hardware. The pressure was on us to stay in the hardware business forever, but we mustered the courage to shift our business to commercial off-the-shelf (COTS) versions of our devices even before the market dictated such a change. The move to COTS hardware meant a complete rethink of both our short-term and long-term strategy. More standardized, but also cheaper, COTS hardware meant we could no longer rely on regular contribution to revenue via hardware refresh as those dollars would not be going to the third-party providers of the off-the-shelf hardware. At the same time, it also meant that we could sell more of our solutions because the lower price point removed a barrier to entry for some and a barrier for expansion for others. It also enabled us to reallocate resources from hardware research and development to software, resulting in a growing library of high-value, high-margin software applications. In the process, we slowly became a software company.

As software has come to dominate our business, it has become an enabler for shifting to a subscription model for delivery of our products. Now our customers can get access to our technology faster and enjoy increased benefits over time with lower up-front costs.

The hard part in all of this? Recognizing these fundamental shifts early—and having the courage to risk everything to pursue them.

Disruption as Freedom

The prospect of disruption can be frightening, but it also is liberating. It means that you simply cannot stick with the status quo, running on inertia. You must meet that disruption head on—and, because you cannot be sure what form this disruption will take, you must scrutinize every part of your company and its operations, asking yourself, "How will the disruption happen here?"

When you have that attitude, and the sense of urgency it induces, you are empowered to make decisions and take actions that you might not do otherwise.

You find yourself questioning the way you have always done things and refusing to accept that "We can't do that," or that "We do not have the right people," or, most dangerous of all, "There's no hurry; we've got time." In the world of business disruption, not only do we not have time, but we are also already behind. Do your 5% and move on to the business accelerator of the next 90%.

Your Early Warning System

First, even if you are proactive about initiating your own disruptions, sometimes you are still going to get hit by an unexpected outside disruption. If you are unlucky, it could wipe you out.

To reduce this likelihood, you must remain eternally proactive, fully aware of what is happening in your industry as well as in the general marketplace. Those print shops had no idea what was about to hit them. Make sure the same thing does not happen to you.

How do you stay vigilant? First, understand the risk of disruption and convey it to your people. Employees have a variety of interests, they have diverse hobbies, and they follow different areas of news. Tell them of the potential for unexpected threats, and reward anyone who spots one early. They are your early warning system, performing sentry duty on the periphery of your organization.

Further, staying close to your customers—who are directly experiencing industry developments—adds to this early warning system. Of course, you may have to endure a slew of false warnings, but that is a small cost to pay for that one item that saves your company.

Just as important, be ready to respond quickly to any competitive threat. Never be complacent.

Even if you do not see it coming, you may still have a brief window of opportunity to respond, even if it means getting out of the business. The 5% Rule is not just about efficiency and productivity; it is also about accelerating mobility and fast adaptation. Bloated, complacent companies, when threatened, are often too slow-moving to react.

By comparison, companies that diligently apply the 5% Rule have a predefined pathway that is flexible enough to enable the organization to pivot on a dime, and in today's business environment, that may prove to be the only strategy you have left.

A Word of Warning About Disruption: Do Not Be Too Clever

The natural assumption about undertaking a company-wide disruption is that you must move even further out along the bleeding edge, to even more arcane and sophisticated technology. The idea is that if you are sufficiently cleverer than the competition—seen and unseen—they will have a harder time keeping up with you.

But there are a couple of problems with that notion. First, adopting more advanced tech is exactly the strategy being taken by your competitors. Chances are they are just as clever and technologically sophisticated as you are. So, leaping ahead may only mean meeting them again on a more difficult field of competition.

Second, there is only so big a technological leap you can make. At any given moment, there is a wall out there—defined by Moore's law and other practical realities—that you cannot get beyond. Not only that, but the closer you get to the wall, the more expensive technological jumps become. The history of high tech is littered with companies whose leaders believed they could leap that wall—and spent themselves into bankruptcies trying to do so.

New tech is not necessarily the answer to your needs, nor the best way to grow revenues. Sometimes you can make a lot more money implementing a low-tech solution or two. Broaden your focus, from changing or evolving your product to looking at every other part of your business. For example, you could change your pricing strategy, offer different deployment models, or even manage contract negotiations in a new way.

Again, the spirit of disruption is that everything is on the table.

I remember reading that Intel, when faced with poor yield rates on its products, took one of its wafer fabrication laboratories and dedicated it to studying every detail of manufacturing to determine what was going wrong. The company, one of the most technologically sophisticated in the world, did not try to implement the newest processes or equipment. Instead, it embarked on a program called "Copy Exactly," in which every action was identified and recorded. A friend told me that the director of the program explained, "I got the idea from McDonald's. I asked myself why McDonald's French fries tasted the same wherever I went. That is why I told my guys, 'We're going to be the McDonald's of semiconductors.'"

It worked.

Thinking Backwards

Finally, one last piece of counterintuitive advice: Be different first, and only then figure out why it is important.

The natural tendency when implementing new processes or products is to figure out what is important to your company, then to determine how that top priority differs from what you currently are doing. From there, you determine what you need to change.

But when it comes to disruption, that top priority may no longer be obvious. Solutions are unknown. Now what matters most is that you are taking off in a new direction—so your priority should rest, first, on being different. Only after you have determined whether a new idea truly is different (and thus disruptive), do you look at whether the idea is, in fact, a worthwhile initiative.

That is how you control your destiny: by cutting a new path and making competitors play your game, instead of vice versa.

Why? Because if you follow the traditional strategy—that is, if you look at importance before novelty to determine your next business initiative, you could find yourself stuck in your current domain, paddling in circles, revising the same old ideas.

Business leaders do not just innovate; they disrupt preemptively, when necessary.

10

The Power of Being Different

Differentiation as a Key Asset

Difference is not just a description, it's a characteristic. It is also a competitive advantage. The trick is, first, to identify the nature of your company's difference, and then determine the value of that difference. Doing so is crucial because it presents an alternate strategy for success.

Regarding the first, how do you identify those features and factors that make your company different? Self-reflection is rarely enough, though it is a good place to start. Ask yourself and your employees, "What makes us special? What distinguishes us from our competitors? From other companies in our community? In other industries?"

Look at your corporate history, your company stories and legends, your iconology and imagery, your corporate culture—what distinguishes them from other companies', especially from your competitors? A word of caution: Your differences may be less obvious than you think. They may hide in the most unexpected places.

Just as none of us really see ourselves as the world sees us, no company knows the complete truth about how the world sees it and its employees. You need to reach beyond self-reflection to gather the opinions of people outside your walls. You may never get the full story, but you will glean some interesting data about people's perceptions. If you are lucky, one of those observations could be the key to leveraging your differences.

A Singular Advantage

Companies often spend millions of dollars on public relations, advertising, and marketing to try to construct an image that distinguishes them from their competitors. Investing millions to call out your differences can be worth it if, and only if, those differences are real.

Those differences must be not just some synthetic difference, like a slightly different shape or name, but unique characteristics that even your competitors cannot challenge. A native difference is more congruent to the real-life culture of your company, and thus less likely to produce contradictions that might disturb customers and strategic partners.

A second benefit of drawing from native differences rather than manufacturing a difference is that native differences already exist. They merely need to be identified and amplified to have the same (or an even greater) impact at a fraction of the cost.

That's the argument for uncovering your actual differences. But what's the value of these differences in the first place? Why do they matter?

Although our commonalities with our competitors make us less visible, our differences help throw us into sharper relief. That enhanced profile, besides saving a considerable amount of money on promotion (not a minor matter in itself) accomplishes something special: it captures attention and gets the ear plugs out before you tell the story.

Being Different Inside

Being different is not just a philosophy for the marketplace. The 5% Rule is itself a powerful differentiator inside a company. Most companies will never be able to put the 5% Rule into practice—much less across the entire company—so those that do will be fundamentally different. And those companies will tend to think differently.

For example, NetScout's use of restricted stock units (RSUs) as an employee incentive has proven to encourage employees with tenure to stay with the company—which in turn results in deep relationships with our customers. Such a plan might never have survived the usual corporate compromises and modifications if its successful implementation hadn't been established by the 5% Rule process at the start.

Different Differences

This brings us back to where we began. First, you identify your difference, and then you determine its value by tracking its influence on the marketplace. Once you determine that value, you'll know whether you should cultivate that difference or abandon it and look for another one.

It may surprise you which of your differences prove to be valuable. For example, at NetScout our product price list is the shortest in our industry. We've kept it that way for several reasons: It enables us to adapt to market changes quickly and simplify the regular disruption process, and it makes the selling process more efficient, which customers appreciate. It also reduces the overhead of maintaining an extended product line, keeping us Lean, even as it trains customers to narrow their orders rather than demand anything and everything.

All of that was planned. What we did not expect was that our shortened product offering would be noticed by the world, for its own sake, and become another way that our current and prospective customers distinguished us from our competitors.

In offering a clear and simple price list, we became "different" without even knowing it. But you can be sure that once we did notice, we capitalized on that difference. For cutting costs and offering fewer products, we have been rewarded with greater profits and more focused customers.

In the 1970s, drawing attention to your difference might not have been important—in fact, being eccentric and idiosyncratic typically hurt companies of that era, especially with investors. But the world has changed: Today there is so much noise in every marketplace that fighting for attention has become a full-time task. Today, it is all about being noticed, and that attention quickly translates into value.

Once your difference comes to define you in the eyes of the market then, in an important sense, you have pioneered a new market—one in which, initially, you are the sole inhabitant—and, when others follow you, the de facto leader. That changes everything.

Instead of being yet another competitor in an increasingly crowded market, you are now the "first mover" in that new market, and first movers get to operate by a whole distinct set of rules. Their attention gets to shift from eking out one tiny slice of market share to maximizing profit margins.

The Tiniest Differences

At this point you may object: Can a difference as minor as a shorter price list really become grounds for announcing that you inhabit a whole new industry, or that you have been unleashed to create your own profit model? This sounds like an overstatement but consider Apple in its early days. The Apple II computer was yet one more of a couple hundred early personal computers. In fact, given Steve Wozniak's brilliant architecture, it had fewer chips and was much cheaper to build than most of its competitors. It was also relatively underpowered, which Wozniak, for all his cleverness, could only partially overcome.

So, the first true Apple computer was a clever but undistinguished product. However, it had some interesting differences. Certainly, there was the odd name and the iconography: the familiar rainbow Apple. But the bigger difference was the packaging: the tan, injection-molded plastic case of the Apple II was both elegant and profoundly different from anything else on the market.

In a world of crude cases made of steel and even wood, Apple stood out sufficiently to overcome the product's other weaknesses.

As we all know, Apple won that first wave of the personal computer revolution, and it has earned premium prices and margins over commodity PCs ever since.

Six years later, the company did it again. This time with the Macintosh, an underpowered computer with insufficient memory, but featuring windows, a bit-mapped display, a graphical user interface, and most of all, a cute one-box design. With the Mac, Apple once again revolutionized home computing. In both cases, a technological generation apart, Apple captured and recaptured dominance over its industry not by being the price or performance leader, but by playing up comparatively minor—but nevertheless decisive—differences. Those differences sufficiently enabled Apple to distinguish itself, permanently, from other companies in its industry.

The company reinforced this advantage with marketing and advertising—including the "Think Different" campaign—that, delivered by the inimitable Steve Jobs, convinced prospective customers to take a closer look. Customers who did also noticed other advantages of the company's computers, notably its incomparable operating system.

Together these features established an intensely loyal customer base, people perpetually hungry for all new things Apple, willing to pay a premium on anything bearing the Apple logo. The resulting margins powered Apple's investment into the creation, in the new century (with Jobs's return to the company), of the company's revolutionary personal technology products—eventually making it the most valuable company in history.

A Caveat

More profits, less competition, and greater control over your destiny—all made possible by being a little bit different from your competitors. Sounds good, doesn't it? But a word of warning. Once again, novelty for its own sake can be a dangerous strategy. For one thing, it can lead you to keep adding functions and features just to distance yourself from your competitors. The history of electronics (and most other industries) is filled with products that failed because they had so many superfluous features that they priced themselves out of their markets or made their products so difficult to use that no one wanted to learn how to do so.

The good news? Difference does not have to be expensive. It does not have to be complicated. Successfully leveraging difference is a subtle process, executed judiciously, not by adding a difference just to be different, but by innovating in ways that both improve customer perception of the product and increase customer appreciation of its value.

In practice, this means that, in the face of a whole universe of features you can add to your product, most will not return their investment, either in revenues or in "difference." In other words, doing nothing is sometimes better than doing something.

Balancing Act

How do you balance novelty, difference, and value? It is a difficult trick. Most companies manage to find a useful difference either by accident or through the eccentricity of a founder, not because they set out to discover one.

The order of action, it turns out, is particularly important to the success of this endeavor: First think of something different to do, then implement it only if it also can be useful. This balancing act can be achieved, and the potential reward always makes the attempt worthwhile.

We have already noted that one way to identify valuable differences—let us call them *subjective differences*—is to survey customers, strategic partners (and we will add the media as well), to cull out those attributes, attitudes, and actions that make a company stand out from the field. Then you can attach a positive or negative value to each of these by empirically testing their impact. If one stands out as having a major and positive impact, you will have identified a powerful competitive tool.

Within your company, you can seek what we might call *objective differences*. We have already discussed features and functions that can be added to our products, and the risk inherent in thinking each additional function or feature will add to the bottom line. The good news is that you do not have to go outside the company (other than for a survey of literature) to find these unique functions and features; you can discover and develop them inside the organization.

Some companies do this work in their R&D departments. Others establish "centers of excellence" that pursue continuous product improvement. What is crucial is that these operations understand the importance of not just improving existing products and discovering new ones but also perpetually searching for features and enhancements that differentiate those products for their own sake. There should be no boundaries to this search.

The group searching for these differences could be a separate team (one featuring representatives from sales, engineering, and product development) that has the power to incorporate the add-ons, or, as we said and cannot emphasize enough, to decide to do nothing at all.

Thus, to find your company's valuable differences, seek both subjective and objective differences, outside and inside your company. Ultimately, as intimidating as the prospect can be, being different—done properly, of course—pays off. Customers do notice the difference; they remember you, and they respect you for it.

CHAPTER

11

Put All Your Eggs in the Fewest Baskets

Balance Risks Without Diluting Rewards

"Don't put all your eggs in one basket." Ever since I first heard that phrase, I have distrusted it. Sure, when it comes to business, pursuing only one product line or market or customer segment is extremely risky behavior. But the phrase only tells you what not to do; it does not say anything about what you should do. For example, putting your eggs in too many baskets would be even riskier.

Furthermore, the advice's attitude is problematic: Not putting all your eggs in one basket is a purely defensive business strategy. It focuses on minimizing risk, not maximizing reward. Except for a period of a disastrous business climate, going on the defensive is a ticket to failure, not success.

The Discipline of Choice

You have heard of stock market strategies that argue you should spread your investment money into as many different stocks—20, 30, more—as you can.

You may wonder, in this case, is not putting your eggs into as many baskets as possible the best way to reduce risk and make money? Yes, you would be reducing risk and making some money. But you will not make much money, while you will be spending valuable time balancing your losses on some stocks with potential profits on other stocks. In the end, it is likely you will not do much better than you would do just sticking your money into a money market fund.

In the stock market and in business ventures, the best strategy is to reduce risk, but only to the point where the return is still high, and you can remain competitive in your industry.

So, how many baskets would that be? If you are a brand-new company, a start-up, you do not have the people, the capital, or the R&D to use more than one basket. That is why entrepreneurship is such a low survival rate activity: A single mistake can kill your company before it has a chance to prove itself, as is the fate of 90% of all start-ups each year.

If you are in a start-up, your greatest chance of long-term success is to get into a second product line, pursue another adjacent market, or grow your customers as quickly as possible, even if this expansion temporarily leaves you a little thin in both operations. A mid-sized company, however, should be well established in at least two businesses and looking for the next one. A company like NetScout, with its $1 billion in revenues, should be in three or four.

Of course, there are many exceptions to this rule out there, and the definition of "baskets" changes at each level of granularity. For example, there is a growing tendency among the biggest technology companies these days—especially those flush with billions of dollars in cash—to embark on dozens of new ventures that have almost nothing to do with their core businesses.

They do so for two reasons. First, bizarrely, lately the stock market has rewarded these side projects with ever-higher stock prices, and thus with more cash to invest in even more projects. Second, it is a natural human tendency not to seek out things to do—that is, not to assert discipline and rigor in the search for a new business for the company's portfolio—but rather to consider anything and everything. Thus, companies may end up with 10 to 20 baskets of new products, technologies, market initiatives, and customer segments.

People justify these tangential businesses, arguing, "Hey, we've got the money," or "It's our proprietary technology/product, so we should take advantage of it," or, most common of all, "It could turn out to be something really big."

What is rarely noticed in all this excitement is that, rather than being free (because the cash is so cheap), these side initiatives are quite expensive. As with maintaining a vast stock portfolio, the hidden cost is the time and talent a company wastes on glittering dead ends, when the best and brightest in the company should be devoting themselves to keeping the company successful in its core businesses.

Side projects will prove even more painfully expensive if the market crashes, all that cash disappears, and the company is stuck trying to shut the side projects down. These fantasy activities are fun during the good times, but they are also quietly sapping the company's immune system. When challenging times hit again, the company's health will be much less resilient.

Lean Basketry

NetScout is a billion-dollar firm with just two business units. Only now, after 25 years, are we going into a third business—a new basket—by adding a new division. Could we have gone into other businesses over the years? Oh yes, many.

Like most companies, we are faced with interesting new opportunities every day. Some may have paid off handsomely, but others might have destroyed us. In the end, by sticking to our principles, and by approaching each of these opportunities with the up-front discipline of the 5% Rule to determine what risks we wanted to take and what choices we wanted to make, we have endured, successfully.

What are our principles on investments and acquisitions? Quite simple. When considering new directions, we make three lists of things we could do. In the first list go all the things that we will not do—initiatives that seem exciting at first but do not fit with our company. This list is the longest but also the least important.

The second list contains items we will do to avoid pushback from our customers. This is a check-off list—what new technological improvements are possible on our existing products, what new relevant features are being offered by our competitors, and what evolutionary advances do our astute customers expect to have soon. This list is of medium length and of medium importance. This we will do because our customers demand them; thus, they take priority over other items and requirements. We must stay profitable and competitive in our existing business by serving our customers.

Finally, the third list contains strategic items driving potential opportunities and company growth—new baskets (as well as enhancements to old baskets) that make sense to consider pursuing. This list is the shortest of the three, but the most important.

It is extremely hard to get onto the third list. In fact, as a rule of thumb, we have only two or three potential initiatives on that list at any one time. As our history shows, it is nearly impossible even for the few items on that third list to be adopted by the company as new initiatives.

It is difficult to choose a smaller number of things to do. It also is quite risky because we have limited the number of ways to win. But we will show you how we make this work later in this chapter. For now, it is important to understand that, in our experience, choosing only a few is still less risky than putting even more bets down and finding your company pulled in far too many directions.

Real-Life Eggs and Baskets

Now, let us stop for a second and take another look at the aphorism that starts this chapter. It is too easy to think of eggs and baskets as a desire to invest in something new and an opportunity that presents itself.

But eggs and baskets are much more complicated than that. In real life, the "eggs" are composed of your people, technology, and intellectual property: your network of strategic partners, your corporate culture, your investors, your existing customers, and your reputation. These are all high-value assets you are about to commit to a new initiative.

Meanwhile, the basket is the market segment you propose to enter, with its unique combination of customer expectations, pricing models, supply and distribution channels, growth rates, competitors, and common business practices. To put some of your eggs into that basket means to shift talent and capital away from your current businesses and to enter a new marketplace which you know less about.

As appealing as this move may be, it is also dangerous. You may want to leap in quickly, before your competitors, but you must restrain yourself from doing so until you have undertaken your 5%, in this case considerable research and deliberation to understand both the market opportunity and the tools you have available to tackle it.

Meanwhile, selecting too many baskets dilutes the good basket and is thus self-defeating. In other words, you must exercise patience and accept a certain amount of delayed gratification while you improve your odds of enjoying a long-term gain. And although that may sound easy, it tends to go against human nature.

I have described how, as we approach a potential company acquisition, I devote most of my time (and that of my acquisition team) at the beginning focusing on whether a deal is worth pursuing at all. By making that decision at the beginning, we spare our company the wasted effort of preparing for something—and of getting committed to something—that will never happen.

Well, the 5% Rule is even more important for new business initiatives. Let us say that there are three ideas on our "must-do" list. Each one represents a major new business opportunity. But each also represents an enormous risk to the company if we pursue it and fail.

As CEO/leader, I see it as my job to investigate each of the three, with the goal of cutting that list down to two, or even one. I investigate the market opportunity, study our resources, and talk to people already in that industry to understand how it operates. After I look at all three, we make the decision.

Note that I have not yet given time to any of the three new business ideas, regarding how we might implement them in the company. I do not want to waste the team's time pursuing dead ends. And I do not want to create advocates and true believers in initiatives that we eventually may have to cancel. That is a morale buster.

If I do pick one initiative, the team will have more than enough to do in the months that follow. But, as the history of our company shows, more often than not, we may pick neither of them, and we'll go back to improving and expanding our current business.

The Unforeseen Cost

Another reason for limiting the number of baskets is that, if left unchecked, every initiative costs more than budgeted. So rather than dealing with a multiplicity of diverse programs, limiting them allows for greater attention and scrutiny.

Over the years, I have learned that the cost of creating new software is always greater than anticipated. There are two reasons for this. First, the original goal of the software, though often straightforward and simple, is soon encrusted with the barnacles of new features, new applications, and endless new lines of code—all in the name of creating a "better" product. The second reason is that code writers, when left to their own devices and to cover any potentially bad code (and perhaps unintentionally to make themselves feel more valuable) write twice as many lines than needed. Put the two together and the resulting mountain of software undermines any original discipline in the product design.

By determining up front what we are not going to do, I have observed that our software developers are now sometimes able to meet the product requirements with up to one-third lines of code as before. The savings in development costs and the improvements in product reliability have been stunning.

Long Road, Hard Wisdom

None of this wisdom came easily. In the early years of the company, like many other founders, I was willing to chase any opportunity that presented itself, especially if our customers wanted it.

Nowadays, it is crucial not to be at the mercy of the whims of others, even our biggest and best customers, but to decide our own fate.

But back at the beginning, we were anxious to get into a second business, both to support and to act as insurance for our primary business. As it happens, we fell in love with the notion of creating a line of security products. Our customers seemed interested, and the new line seemed complementary to our original line of service assurance products.

It was not long before we realized that we had made a mistake. The lesson we quickly learned (and have never forgotten) is this: Just because two industries look complementary, that does not mean they are. In retrospect, we made four major mistakes:

- We got anxious. We felt like we needed a second product line, but that did not mean we needed one. In fact, with a little more thought we would have realized that we were being premature; we had neither the time nor the financial resources to pursue such an initiative at that stage. We even tried to make up for this with a small acquisition.

- We fell in love. This was one of the reasons why I developed the 5% Rule. At no point—especially at the beginning—did I make a go/no go decision on the project. Rather, the initiative quickly began to take on a life of its own, until it became unstoppable. Once we found a candidate in the industry for acquisition, it was already too late. The deal's momentum was impossible to stop.

- We had the wrong reasons. Though we did not want to admit it to ourselves, the real reason we wanted to get into this new business was to make up for the weaknesses in our current business.

Instead, we made it worse. Because our first product line was not doing so well, instead of fixing the underlying issue we tried to generate more revenues through the second segment, which could have hastened the demise of our core business.

- We were not realistic. Looking back over the years, it is obvious now that we did not do our due diligence on the security market. If we had, we would have realized that although it looked like our current business, it did not operate like it. In fact, we could not just extend our current functions into this market but had to build a whole new infrastructure—sales, support, channels, everything.

The result was the only acquisition in NetScout's history that had to be jettisoned. This painful memory still bothers me. Yet, through it I learned some of the lessons presented in this book. Interestingly, several years later, we once again added a new basket in the security space, but this time for the right reasons, resulting in successful outcomes.

Timing Is Everything

As I write this, after several decades of operating in two baskets, NetScout is investing in a third. Why? Because we believe it is the right time to do so, which should always be your criteria.

At the same time, we have made a calculated choice to shift from revenue growth to profit in the short term. This has meant cutting back on certain product lines and operating expenses. We have made decisions only after considerable thought, research, and communication with our customers—the 5%. Now our team has the guardrails it needs to freely execute, and with the long-term direction and end goal in mind, they are racing to fully implement this new software initiative.

This initiative will be disruptive to our company as it exists now. But as you have just read, disruption can be a good thing; you need to disrupt yourself before the market does it for you.

Selling software is our disruption, and it will surprise our competitors, which will give us an advantage.

How will our customers react? Our shareholders? Both, in my experience, will resist the new basket, in the beginning. Neither wants change, so although both customers and shareholders initially may think they are serving our interests, they can in fact be a drag on our ability to remain successful.

What they really do not want is increased risk. That is understandable. So, we need to explain to both constituencies why we are making this change.

To the shareholders, the message needs to be that the risk is even greater if we stick with the status quo and let the disruption happen to the company, rather than taking command over our own fate. To customers, it means that we can serve them even better in the future. To both, it means showing them that we have a detailed plan for changing the wheels of the company, even while it is racing down the road.

12

Don't Worry About Leaving Money on the Table

Get What You Need, Not What You Want

Much of the unhappiness in the world, I believe, stems from a dynamic that comes into play during the last 10% of business negotiations. This is why business dealings are often so frustrating. We go into them unprepared, we have nebulous goals for how they should end, and we walk away worried that we have somehow been snookered into leaving money on the table that should now be in our pockets.

This frustration does not come up just in financial transactions. Think about the times you have been presented with several options—advertising campaigns, color schemes, marketing strategies, job candidates—and been asked to decide. How often do you fear, up front, that you will make the wrong choice? How often, afterwards, do you worry that you were not given enough options, that the perfect choice is still out there somewhere?

As I mentioned previously, I am astounded by how many companies enter merger negotiations with NetScout—deals sometimes worth hundreds of millions of dollars—without any idea how much they are worth or how much they really want. Their operating principle seems to be, "Let's find out how much NetScout will pay for us, and if we like the number, we'll ask for just a little more."

That's not a good negotiating strategy; it is simply wishful thinking. It is also a terrible way to start a long-term business relationship. Why do we want to merge with another company into ours when we know that the management of that company either thinks they ripped us off or is bitter because they think we did the same to them?

That is why one of my primary tasks in the first 5% Rule is to establish a price. If the other side is not going to do it, then I am going to do it.

The price I set is not based on trying to lowball the other side to see what we can get away with. Rather, it is determined by what we think the other company is worth. This process requires deep research: We talk to industry analysts, study the company's balance sheet, investigate its intellectual property portfolio, look at new products in development, talk to customers, and on and on. We also consider what contribution that company could make to the bottom line, as part of NetScout.

So, when we go back to that company, we are armed with an offer price that can be empirically justified. We are not trying to bluff, nor intimidate, nor rope-a-dope on the other side; on the contrary, we are stating the price we are willing to pay.

Now, here is the thing: We may not care what the other side wants. We know what we want, and that is the figure we give them. If the other party does not think it is enough, then likely there will be no deal. That is unfortunate, but once we know the value of the deal, why would we deviate far from it? However, if our number is more than the other side is expecting, then it is good for them. It is a bonus: It will make them even happier with the deal and with us in our work together. If we green light the merger, then we will have satisfied new employees.

My point is that if we know the right deal for us, why should it matter if we could have gotten a better deal? Sure, in theory, we will have "money left on the table," but I challenge even that assumption. It is easy to focus on the money we had saved; but in my experience, that kind of thinking also underestimates the actual costs.

Let us say our only goal was to get the lowest price. So, we took advantage of the other side, and we got the best deal we could. Then what? We bring into the company, in many cases into positions of authority, people whose only taste of NetScout has been bitter and who feel aggrieved. Tell me, how much do we have to save on that deal to make up for the ultimate cost of a dysfunctional relationship with our new cohort of employees? I would say that even if we got the other company for free, it would not be worth it.

That is why I say that determining what you want beforehand, then settling for that result without worrying about what you did not get, is the essence of both Lean and Not Mean. It is Lean because once you have determined, using the 5% Rule, the price you want, then everything beyond that is just a waste of time. Months of negotiating only burns up valuable time, and that is hardly Lean. Wasting time afterwards regretting what you left on the table is also not Lean; your job is to look ahead, not back.

Meanwhile, this approach is also Not Mean. Bringing in new employees who feel like the deal was fair and who feel welcomed into the company as equals is the most positive, affirming, and morale-inducing thing you can do. This is why we bring new employees up to the same compensation and benefit levels as NetScout. This positivity reaches beyond these new team members to the new customers you are gaining as well because they can feel when morale drops among the folks with whom they have always dealt.

A happy acquisition is a healthy acquisition. Why acquire a company that you have just made toxic?

Counting What You Do Not Have

It is human nature to fear that we are being cheated out of what is rightfully "ours" or, conversely, to fear that, through our own indecision or tentativeness, we are not getting every bit that we deserve.

Think about this in your own life. You go to a dealership to buy a car, and you find yourself in negotiations with a salesperson. Eventually you settle on a price, but as you walk out you get that gnawing feeling in your gut that if you had been just a little cleverer, you might have gotten a better deal, or that the salesperson is laughing at you because he took you to the cleaners.

The solution? Know what you want, get it, and do not look back. Let me explain.

In 2001, during the dot-com crash, thousands of people in the technology industry let their fear of missing that last dollar destroy them financially. Tragically, just one slight change in their behavior would have made them wealthy, set for life. Instead, many were left bankrupt; some even lost their homes.

Here is what happened: under the US tax code, if you own corporate stock options, the tax you owe is based on the stock price of those options when you exercise them. In other words, if your options cost $.10 to exercise, and the market price that day is $100, then your tax is set at $100 per share.

Fair enough. But in the go-go days of the internet bubble, a whole lot of people owned thousands of shares, with an exercise value of just a few bucks, but a market value of tens of millions.

Given the growing volatility of the market during that period, many people went ahead and exercised their options so that they could sell the stock quickly and take advantage of the growing bubble before it popped. Many of them exercised their options, but rather than selling immediately, they chose to hold them for a year so they could pay long-term capital gains tax and avoid paying ordinary income tax. It seemed a clever strategy, except for one fatal flaw: Most people did not have a clear idea what their stock should be worth. All they really knew, based on the price inflation of the previous few years, was that it should be worth as much as possible. In other words: It should be worth more.

When the dot-com industry did start collapsing, and the stock market began to crash, too many people made the wrong decision to just hang on a little longer and cash out at the next peak, not because they had any empirical evidence that stock prices would rise again soon, but because, in their eyes, the shares should be worth what they were at their peak. In their minds, they wanted, indeed they were owed, that last 10% back.

Of course, they never got it. In fact, other than a few small bumps, most of those stocks fell continuously for the next year, annihilating 90% of the start-ups of the dot-com boom. Those shareholders? They watched as their paper evaporated, hundreds of billions of dollars of stock value, up in smoke.

Worse, they still owed the IRS taxes on the options they had executed and not sold. That is how many people lost just millions they never had, but now, thanks to taxes, millions they did have. Hello, bankruptcy.

It is easy to dismiss this behavior as simple greed, and surely greed comes into it. But it is more complicated than that. The best way to describe it is "magical thinking"—the idea that what we wish to come true is destined to come true, that we are somehow due a reward, even if no evidence of that duly exists.

This same "magical thinking" is what drives us to enter negotiations armed with a conviction of our goal and the intention of only getting what we need.

Different Tables

Note that, so far, I have dealt only with the acquisition. But a willingness to leave "money"—or its equivalent—on the table works in other parts of business as well. Take for example, our Guardians of the Connected World marketing campaign. This new branding initiative was created by a team that included both company marketers and an outside consultant. I asked our team to take some time, ponder, and come back with alternatives for this campaign.

When the day came, they sat me down and began their presentation of various alternative ideas. I listened to their first idea, and I told them I did not like it. Then they presented their second idea, Guardians. I listened, then said, "I like it. We will go with that one."

As you can imagine, they were surprised. They had prepared an elaborate presentation with a half-dozen creative and appealing ideas. "Don't you want to see the rest? Don't you want to look at all the choices?"

"Why?" I responded. "I've got what I like."

Now, my response may seem odd to many readers. But here is my reasoning: What if I had sat there and spent another hour listening to the rest of their presentation? What would I have gained? I already had what I needed or wanted. Everything else was superfluous. At worst, listening to more presentations might have distracted me from making the right choice. At best, there may have been another branding idea so dazzling that it would have overwhelmed Guardians of the Connected World.

What then? It would have been just another campaign that would also have met our goals. But I did not need two campaigns; I already had one that not only hit the mark as a marketing campaign but also so perfectly expressed our sense of duty to our industry and our customers that we eventually adopted it as our identity and statement of our higher ambition.

At the time, some of the teams were a bit put out by my abrupt decision. They wanted to show off their brilliant ideas. But I already knew they had brilliant ideas; that is why they were selected for the team. I already trusted them to make the right choices, and they had just proven to me that they did.

Should I have listened to the rest of the presentations, picked two or three finalists, and then sent the team away to work for another couple of weeks, only to come back to me and stage a run-off competition? What would we have gained? How would that have been efficient? And how would making some of our most talented employees compete against each other, leading some to waste their time, been an effective use of resources?

No, I decided on the spot, and then executed quickly. It proved an enormous success, and I do not regret what I never got to see. Magical thinking wins again.

Similarly, this approach applies to product pricing and discounting. Pricing has become something of a black art, with companies using all sorts of algorithms and computer programs to figure out, down to the last quarter cent, how a new product should be priced and how much an established product should be discounted for different customers. The goal here, as always, is to squeeze out maximize revenues. You feed in cost of goods sold and a bunch of other variables, and your algorithm spits out the number that enables the best profit margin.

But does it? At NetScout we do just the opposite. We use the 5% Rule to establish the proper margin on our products—across the entire product line—and that margin determines the price. It is fast, simple, and Lean. It is also one reason we do not believe in "loss leader" products. Beyond the fact that they sacrifice margins for market share (which rarely translates back to restored profits), they add complexity and time to the company pricing model.

Know Your Price

Ah, but you may be asking, what if presetting margins means leaving 30%, or 40%, or even 50% of the potential profit on the table?

My first answer is, so what? If we know the price we want, and we get it, we have done our job. Besides, what if the market is more elastic than you thought—a phenomenon that sometimes occurs when the economy shifts. That 40% higher price may just drive away more customers than you anticipated. However, a right (lower) price may drive more pervasive use and hence bigger deals.

My second answer is, once you have got the price you want, and everything beyond that stays with your (delighted) customer, the payback comes in intangible, but often important, ways, like goodwill, loyalty, upgrades, and all sorts of other benefits that can get you through challenging times. That is a lot better than holding out for some imagined "best deal" now.

Quick, smart decisions start with the 5% Rule—by doing the work to understand what you really want. When you go into a room knowing what you want, and your counterpart does not, you always win. When you do not care what you leave on the table once you have gotten what you want, life becomes much easier, and your success rate much higher. When you finally realize—unlike those stock option holders—that there is no absolute best, only what you think is best, you inoculate yourself against potential disaster.

State What You Want

How do you convey what you want to the other side of the negotiating table? You tell them.

In the tech industry, typically you ask your sales team to deliver their numbers by using all the products and solutions available to them. The assumption is that the more products they try to sell, the better the result. At NetScout, we do a 5% meeting with the account manager for key accounts, understand all the avenues for sale at that account, and then pick one key initiative to drive with the customer. This results not only in the customer not getting overwhelmed but also realizes the best outcome for them and us.

Tech companies also typically write a market requirements document (MRD), then a product requirements document. At NetScout we add an additional step. To make sure there is no disconnect between the stakeholders we have introduced what we call a *pre-MRD*: a one-page crisp definition of the problem statement. The why? is clearly explained without ever looking at the market size and numbers.

Know When to Stop

Let me end this chapter with an Indian folk tale that reveals the difference between negotiating for a specific outcome and negotiating for a "better deal."

A man from a village in India planned to travel to the big city for the first time in his life. Concerned, he went to the worldliest man in his village, who had traveled to many cities, and asked him, "What do I have to know to survive in the city?"

"Ah," said the man, "What you need to know is that negotiation is a big problem the city. Price is an important thing. So just keep one thing in mind. When they say, 'Ten rupees,' you say 'Five.' Always offer half of the quoted price. That is it. Just remember that."

So, the villager headed for the city, carrying a big basket he hoped to fill with mangoes to bring home. As he entered the farmers' market, he saw stall after stall of grocers selling beautiful, ripe mangoes.

Not sure how to proceed, the villager went to the first stall and told the vendor that he wanted to buy a basket full of mangoes. "How much is it?" he asked.

The vendor studied the villager, then said, "One hundred rupees."

The villager, remembering what he had been told, replied, "No I want it for 50 rupees."

"No sale," said the vendor.

Undeterred, the villager went to the next booth and asked to buy a basket of mangoes. That vendor, who had overhead the previous conversation, said, "Fifty rupees."

"No," said the villager, remembering the advice, "I want it for 25 rupees."

Angry, the vendor told him to move on.

And so, it continued. At each new stall, the vendor agreed to the price the villager had demanded at the previous stall, only to be told that the man now would agree only to half that price. At each stall, the village man was turned away.

Finally, the man reached the last stall selling mangoes. The vendor had heard the man coming, so when the village man asked about the price of mangos, the vendor replied, "Look, we are all getting tired of your little game. Just fill your basket with my mangoes. They are free."

The villager, pleased that his strategy had worked so brilliantly, replied, "I want two baskets." The vendor looked at him, calculating, and replied, "Okay. Two baskets. But I still need some to sell. So, leave these here, and you will have to get your two baskets of mangoes the same way I did."

"How?" asked the villager.

"It's easy," the vendor replied, "I get my mangoes for free from a tree. I climb up the tree in the morning, pick the mangoes, and bring them here. My price is based on my labor. Just follow me and you can harvest the ripest ones for yourself."

So, the two walked five miles to the edge of the city to find the tree, laden with mangoes. But it was a very tall tree. "No problem," said the vendor, who walked behind some rocks and came back with a rickety ladder. "Now," he said, "up you go."

The villager climbed high in the tree. He quickly filled his first basket and started to climb down to get the other basket. But when he looked down, he discovered that the vendor had removed the ladder. The village man shouted down, "How do I get down?"

"That's a problem, isn't it?" said the vendor.

"Help, help!" the villager shouted. But his voice only echoed.

"There's no one here but me," said the vendor. "But I'll tell you what: I'll take 200 rupees to get you down."

After a long while thinking, the villager agreed to pay the 200 rupees for his lesson in negotiations.

13

Communication Disconnects at the Top
Clarity Equals Productivity

A s I approach the last couple of chapters of this book, I would like to cover the subject that under-pins both the 5% Rule and the Lean But Not Mean philosophy that it helps make possible. It is also the most important beneficiary of both those practices: communications.

A company that communicates well internally, from top to bottom, across operating groups, and out to stakeholders, is one that can operate at the highest levels of efficiency and do so in the most humane and enlightened way.

But most companies do not do that, even when they implement the most sophisticated information-sharing apparatus and hire the most expensive consultants to facilitate their new and improved communications program. Why doesn't it work? I think in most cases it is because they may have the communications model backwards, and then they blame the wrong people for the failure.

Talk to most companies and they will tell you that their biggest communications problem is that the rank-and-file employees just do not seem to get the message, no matter how clear they make it, or how many times they repeat it. Implicit in this complaint is that the folks on the bottom of the organization chart are just too unmotivated to listen.

Of course, these senior managers and executives do not have that problem. Just ask them: to a person they will tell you that they are superior communicators. Their proof? That they have reached such an exalted position in the company. They must be great communicators, right?

Let me tell you one of the most important things I have learned over the years: If a company has a communication problem, it always starts with disconnections at the higher layers of the organization.

Babel

How can this be? Simple. I was once in a meeting in which all four of our senior executives agreed on a course of action. That would seem to be the result you want: equanimity with everyone on the same page. It should be easy then to announce this decision through the organization, with little fear of confusion, right?

But just out of curiosity, I decided to finish the meeting by asking my counterparts why they wanted to follow this course of action. Each of them gave a different reason. In other words, our apparent agreement on the strategy was just a thin skin over profound differences in our points of view or motivations, and our notions about how this strategy should be executed.

Given that confusion with just five people, it would be foolish to imagine that, in turn, those four executives could present that plan to hundreds of employees without sowing even more confusion. What we assumed was effective communication would have seemed to our employees to be wildly divergent, even contradictory, messages. Yet, who would have been blamed for the resulting confusion? The employees, of course.

One of the biggest complaints in many organizations is that intergroup communications—that is, between business units, departments, divisions, facilities, and so forth—are constantly breaking down. This failure is always blamed on the inability (or unwillingness) of these entities to speak to each other. They are jealous of each other, or they are competing to get ahead of the other, or they care more about their own organization's health over the health of the whole company—the breakdown is always blamed on some form of bad faith by the people involved.

Some companies seem to go crazy trying to solve this problem. They hold reconciliation meetings between the two business units; they threaten punishment if they do not get along; and, most notoriously, they go out and hire expensive consultants to act as intermediaries between the warring parties. Of course, nothing ever seems to work.

I used to believe all this, too, until I noticed two things. First, employees in both camps, outside of these breakdowns over "official" communications, seemed to get along quite well. Unofficially, they worked well together, everyone tried to do their jobs well, and all were loyal and dedicated to the success of the company.

The second thing I noticed was that whenever there was a communications breakdown between two business entities, there was also a similar communications breakdown within one or both.

This difference between official and unofficial behavior, and the correlation between internal and external communications failures, could not be a mere coincidence. So, I wondered, what if we were attacking this problem backwards? What if we were merely treating symptoms and not the disease?

That proved to be a turning point. The more I looked at the internal communications of these business groups or departments, the more I saw the same dynamic playing out across the company: the same illusory agreement on top of the same mixed signals. These business groups or departments could not communicate well with their counterparts, largely because they could not even manage to communicate well with themselves.

Now, add another wrinkle to this. At any given time, between any two business groups, there are rarely more than three or four points of contact. What happens when those contacts cannot agree with each other on their message or purpose? Communications breakdown. Is it any wonder these business groups are not aligned?

Misalignment may be the best-case scenario. Much worse is the natural human reaction to mixed messages—simply to shop around and choose the answer you want. Now, instead of the two business units not knowing what each other wants, they instead operate on what they want the other's position to be. As a result, the two operations begin actively to undermine each other.

That is the kind of mess that makes parent company management throw up its hands and call in an expensive outside consultant, who calls a temporary truce, puts a bandage on the problem, and leaves behind a big bill. Within weeks, the two business units are back to their old ways, until senior management again throws up its hands, announces that it simply cannot deal any more with such incompetence, and starts replacing division or department managers, never digging in to understand what created this mess.

Clarity Comes First

Let me repeat the title of this chapter: "Communication Disconnects at the Top"—that is, disconnects begin with the leadership at each level of the company. Executive row creates and then reinforces dysfunctional corporate communications by not establishing clarity from the very beginning. This dysfunctionality flows down through the organization, often picking up speed as it goes, and creating confusion along the way.

That is just the vertical impact. When the messaging needs to go sideways between business units, the confusion multiplies. Then, as the final straw, senior management punishes lower-level employees for their apparent incompetence.

These communications breakdowns explain why companies become less competitive as they get bigger.

The will is there, people still work smart and hard, but the head and the feet can no longer communicate with each other intelligently.

So, How Do You Solve This Problem?

Top management needs to communicate more precisely and in unison, both what they are doing and why. This does not mean micromanaging the company; I mean that when you make decisions, do not settle for mere agreement on the message. Instead, you must agree also on motives and methods.

For example, it is not enough to agree on raising R&D expenditures next year; you must also agree on why you are doing so, and how you intend to act on this decision.

Of course, this means you must make real decisions, up front, beyond setting the company's direction. How? Ah, now we are back to the 5% Rule. In fact, it has often crossed my mind that the real purpose of the 5% Rule is to clarify organizational communications. It forces you, as the person responsible, to make real decisions, right now, at the beginning of the process. When this process is executed properly and completely, the message becomes clear and unambiguous: We are doing this, for this reason, in this way.

The clearer the message communicated at the top of the organization, the less fuzzy it gets as it moves down through the organization. If the 5% Rule has become universal in a company, then ever-more precise decision-making and communication take place as the company's plans are disseminated throughout the organization.

Done correctly, all business units will speak with one clear voice. At every point of contact, the message will be the same. There will be no ambiguity, no confusion, no cross-purposes.

This communication structure too will be Lean. No more desperate hiring of consultants, no more feuding business units, no more wasted time trying to clear up the confusion created by disconnected communications. This strategy could enable big companies to behave much "smaller" and to grow nimbler, just as it could help smaller companies grow much faster.

Of course, this strategy is also much less Mean. Nothing makes employees angrier than feeling betrayed or blamed for something they know they did not cause. This frustration is only exacerbated when they sense that the people blaming them are also responsible. To paraphrase President Lincoln, "A company divided against itself cannot stand."

A company filled with employees who feel they are not getting a fair deal is one that will not survive overall.

Beyond Mean

The 5% Rule makes possible clear and precise communications. Together with honest dealings with employees and all other stakeholders, as well as the right priorities (including decisiveness and trust), the 5% Rule makes it possible to build a Lean company that treats its employees in an enlightened, Not Mean way.

It has taken me 30 years as a CEO, and many mistakes along the way, to understand all of this. I wish I had figured it out decades ago. But somehow, we survived, and we can now make NetScout the great company it was meant to be. Initially, I drafted this book to codify this philosophy for our employees and my successors, but just as important, I want to share this with others:

- Employees are inevitably blamed for not understanding instructions or assignments. But in every case the real problem is with their manager providing inaccurate, incomplete, or contradictory messages. Look for this cause before settling on blame.

- The best way to fight communication disconnects is to not only send information from the top-down in the corporation but also to establish better feedback loops from the bottom-up—and then immediately intervene if the two do not agree.

14

Primary and Secondary Skills

Prepare Careers for the Future

Finally, a chapter on individual productivity, a necessary contributor to the successful implementation of the 5% Rule.

Why do some high performers—in business, politics, and life—maintain optimal performance throughout their lives, and others, some of whom possess even greater talent, quickly fade, and fall behind? And why do some lesser performers suddenly take off in mid-career and accomplish astonishing things?

The standard answer is this: Some people are sprinters and others are long-distance runners. Some burn out early, and others learn to pace themselves.

I do not believe this for minute. These may be symptoms, but they are not root causes. What experience has taught me, and I have only been able to formulate this recently, is that your primary skills—those talents by which you earned your college degrees and first made your professional reputation—can take you only so far.

After that, it is your secondary skills—those capabilities, often underrated, like your ability to interact effectively with others—that define your career. The mistake most companies, and individual employees themselves, make is to focus their efforts only on primary skills, minimizing the importance of secondary skills—though, in the end, those secondary skills are much more important.

Primary School

Let me explain. Primary skills are those talents, aptitudes, and abilities that you grow up with. They lead you to the thing you know you want to be for the rest of your life: chemist, software engineer, pilot, salesperson, or any of a thousand other careers. This is what you study in school to put you on the path to a profession. When you finally start your career, primary skills are the centerpiece of your job. They are what you do, how you define yourself to the world, how you grow your network of professional contacts. Your performance in this primary skill area is how your employer judges you with raises and promotions.

In the early years of your professional career, you work extremely hard at your primary talent, and you are rewarded for your efforts. The pathway ahead seems clear: Just keep getting better at what you do. Forever.

But then, as you approach the first decade in your career, you notice two troubling things. First, getting better is getting to be a whole lot harder. Giant leaps of improvement in your skills, which used to come easily in your apprentice years, now are almost impossible. The gains are smaller and more incremental.

By about the 15-year mark in your, say, 30-year career, especially if you are a top performer, even those small gains begin to disappear. This is hardly a mark of failure, it is a measure of success, and of near mastery. You are now at the top of your game. It was easy to go from 20% to 40% performance at the beginning of your career; now it is much, much harder to go from, say, 94% to 95%. You are facing the "diminishing returns syndrome."

For many top performers, this career plateau can be deeply dispiriting. Many assume that they will just keep getting better at their primary skill for the rest of their working lives.

But now they have hit a ceiling, and they face the disturbing prospect either of being overtaken—or even replaced—by those behind them, or of changing their career trajectory.

This moment in a person's career can present a severe problem for the employer of one of these high-fliers. For years, the company has depended on this person's ever-improving talent. Now, though this person is still a top performer—in the laboratory, in sales, in design, in code writing—the continuous improvement in their skills has waned.

Just as a successful company that is now growing in only low single digits can become a cause for investor concern, a demotivated, peaked-out employee can suffer a substantial reduction in their productivity, causing concern for their employer.

Double Lives

It was in pondering this crisis in our employees—indeed, in my own career—that I had an epiphany: we have two careers.

The first is defined by, and builds on, our primary skills. But as much as we wish otherwise, most of us run through that career in about 15 years or so, or approximately half of our professional lives. The more talented a person is, the more likely this turning point will occur. And it really is a turning point because our secondary skills are radically different than our primary ones.

Always secondary skills involve interpersonal skills, ranging from leadership to taking on the new goal of making others successful. This transition can be a gut-wrenching experience, and it explains why a mediocre technologist can sometimes become a great corporate executive, and the superstar scientist can ruin their reputation by becoming a lousy boss.

There is some truth to that old cliché about the A student working for the B student, but only because the B student made better use of their secondary skills during that second phase of their career.

Our primary skills are typically learned in an academic setting, during a brief period of our lives, then polished through application.

Secondary skills are acquired over many years, through life experience and working with mentors. Further, primary skills are additive, while secondary skills are multiplicative. That is why, as you approach the 15-year employment mark, it is so hard to add that next tiny incremental improvement in your primary skills. When you improve your secondary skills, however, you have a multiplicative effect: You are not just improving your own productivity but also that of the people around you, particularly your subordinates, but also your peers and colleagues. Thus, you might struggle, in your primary skill, to progress from 93 to 94 on a scale of 1 to 100, but applying your secondary skills to yourself and your direct reports can create a jump to 180 or 270 or more.

That is why great leaders are so valuable, and why a leader's value continues to increase, even after their primary skills growth exists solely to understand the work of others, to lead them effectively.

When my cofounder and I first started NetScout, one of the reasons we were so effective was that our skills were complementary. In the terms of this chapter, his primary skills were my potential secondary skills. I was the technologist, he the businessperson. But now, after years of leading the company as its CEO, even he will agree that I have inherited most of his primary skills as my secondary skills. However, there are many 30- or 40-year-olds in the company who now far eclipse me when it comes to being a pure technologist.

Sometimes a secondary skill can be meeting management. Or communicating effectively in speeches or memos. Or managing multitiered advancement among scores of employees at distinct levels of age, experience, expertise, and performance. Just today, as I write this, I managed the negotiation of a site license agreement with one of the world's largest corporations. I did not need that skill at age 30, but I certainly need it now.

Making the Turn

This brings us to an interesting question: When exactly should you start developing your secondary skills or cultivating them in others who work for you?

It may seem that you should do so from the start, but I disagree. You might study speech in high school or take some accounting courses in college, but the reality is that once you enter the workforce your focus should be to perfect your primary skills as much as possible. That is where you will find the most successful and best position yourself for the second phase of your career.

Unfortunately, many of the most talented employees, and the most enlightened employers, fail to see the truth of that. Instead, employers try to promote people early—too early—into management. That is a mistake, because they will not realize the full accomplishment of the skills that have defined their lives to this point, and instead they will be off on a new path for which they are unprepared.

For companies, this is also a mistake because they have not yet gotten the full primary productivity out of those employees, yet those employees have been transferred to a new line of work that will take them years to perfect. Note that the multiplicative effect really happens when the secondary skills act as a multiplier to maximize primary skills.

However, if you wait too long to begin cultivating those secondary skills—either through education or on-the-job training—you run a different kind of risk.

Remember the Peter Principle? It was the idea, first promulgated by management theorists in the 1960s, that people were promoted upwards in an organization until they reached their "level of incompetence." The Peter Principle was partly tongue-in-cheek, but everyone recognized that it also contained a lot of truth. Promoting too early can be both wasteful and cruel.

To my mind, the Peter Principle may have been the first recognition of what happens when you fail to prepare a successful employee for the second phase in their career. It is the unfortunate example of the company superstar who is "rewarded" by being promoted from the lab or field sales to a management job, only to fail miserably at it. The most horrifying examples of this are the brilliant employees who are suddenly thrust into a vice presidency—or even the CEO's chair—who then put the entire company at risk.

You need only to glance at the financial pages to see that this kind of disaster happens all the time. So, how do you deal with the ambitious young employee who wants a quick promotion into management? Or the company's top scientist or number one salesperson who is beginning to peak at their specialty?

I do not have all the answers yet. As I have said, I have only recently come to this understanding about the two phases of people's careers. But my sense is that for the ambitious first-phase person, you need to act as a brake to keep them from making a shift they may come to regret. One way to do that is to keep giving them ever-greater challenges in their primary skill and both rewarding and honoring them when they accept those challenges and succeed. Yes, you may lose a few who just cannot wait and take a management position somewhere else. But when that happens, remember that you are not losing that primary talent, because they were not going to pursue it anymore.

As for the veteran, the solution is different. You must track their progress. If the usual primary career is 15 years, then sometime about the 10-year mark you, as their boss, should sit down with that individual and begin plotting that next phase in their career. Then embark on a five-year plan to train and transition them one step at a time into that new role. If they choose to stay with their primary skills and leave for another company, well, they were about to peak anyway. If you did try to turn them into managers, they might have been destructive to the organization.

However, if they do agree to the transition, you have a half-decade to make them as top-notch in their future career as they are in their current one. This is management that is the essence of Not Mean. And, because you started early, it also follows the 5% Rule.

Once again, keep in mind that every person is different. So far, I have treated primary skills as technical ones. But there are also people in your organization who have trained as managers, such as people who have earned their MBAs. This does not mean they escape the destiny to have a two-phase career. But rather, compared to the technical folks, they might even take a reverse path, spending their second phase devoted to applying their business skills to becoming sufficiently knowledgeable about technology to be able to lead the company.

The Next Dimension

Now, I hesitate to even discuss this, because my thinking is still so preliminary, but I am increasingly coming to believe that there is, in fact, a tertiary skill. Unconsciously, I have always known it—I've even, in brief periods of my life, like most people, experienced it—but only now has it come to the surface in my thinking.

This third "skill," if that is the right word, if you are lucky, may enable you to discover your genius. This skill is vastly different from the other two. For one thing, it does not follow sequentially after the first two, but can happen at any time—if you are lucky, multiple times—in your career. It runs in parallel to the other two skills, invisible, waiting for the opportunity to emerge. If your primary skill is additive, and your secondary skill is multiplicative, your third skill is exponential. Sometimes I wonder if the tertiary skill is simply reaching your maximum potential—maximized primary skills multiplied by maximized secondary skills. This is when your career rockets into the stratosphere, when you make your mark on the world.

"Discovering your genius" is not just "finding your calling." It is much bigger than that. It is like discovering a fourth dimension to what you do.

How do you know you have achieved that heightened plane? I believe it is when you surprise yourself at what you can do. No one can, or needs to, tell you when that moment will occur (but they may very well notice the result). You must find that moment in yourself and then take advantage of it, accomplishing things that seem superhuman.

I have had those heightened moments only recently in my career. Odds are you have as well. It is an amazing feeling; you just cannot believe what you are able to do. Suddenly it seems as if, effortlessly, you can do things better and faster than you ever have before. Athletes call it being "in the zone," actors and writers call it "reaching a higher plane," programmers sometimes describe it as being "wired" or "thinking in code."

Typically, it does not last long—often it has gone before you even know what happened—and you are left dreaming of the day that lightning will strike again. If you are lucky, it does.

One of the hardest things for an entrepreneur to do is to make the transition from life in a start-up to CEO of a maturing company. That is why very few public corporations still have their founders at the helm. But among those that do, I believe, all are led by entrepreneurs who have developed their secondary skills as a multiplier—and then reached that higher plane.

Planning Ahead

How does all this relate to the 5% Rule?

Managing your employees by recognizing this fundamental shift in the middle of their careers is the very essence of Lean decision-making. It overcomes the wasteful process of having employees taking on tasks for which they are unprepared, or leaving too early from jobs for which they still have years of added productivity. This failure to make a successful shift deprives the company of some of its most valuable talent. Instead, a smooth transition saves time, money, and people.

It is also perpetuates a Not Mean culture because allowing a young employee to transition early without fulfilling their primary talents is unfair. Even more callous is taking an extraordinarily successful employee at the midpoint of their career and tossing them into a management role for which they are unprepared, and then letting them fail.

No, an enlightened, people-first company tracks all of its employees, identifies where each of them are in their careers at any given moment, supports their professional development, and then, as they approach their career turning point, prepares them—with added duties, training, and a mutually agreed-on strategy—to make that transition successfully. This is no trivial task. It requires a whole host of people, from HR to departmental leadership, to orchestrate. It is exactly this type of endeavor, made complex by the participation of multiple departments, its application to all employees, and its perpetual duration, that benefits the most from the application of the 5% Rule. The discipline and guardrails that the 5% Rule provides ensures that no matter which department has an action, the long-term objective of developing the next generation of leaders is met. This can also lead to efficient, targeted succession planning.

The saying: "throw someone in the deep end and the best will survive" is foolish and limiting. I say, "throw someone in the deep end only when you believe that they can survive." When you challenge people with greater responsibility—and know with 100% certainty that they will prevail—you no longer must micromanage their work. But the real benefit is that trust gives the other person the opportunity to surprise you with just how capable they are.

Maturing
a Great Company
Create the Next Generation of Leaders

I n theory, companies can stay young forever. But the reality is that even the greatest companies grow old and fade away. You only look at any list of leading companies in each field in one decade, and then same list in the next decade, and see how few survive.

But if enterprises do have a lifespan, it is hard to predict what it is. There have been billion-dollar high-flyers, such as Silicon Graphics and Sun Microsystems, that have seemed to dominate their corner of the business world and that were gone a dozen years later. And yet there are other companies that are still thriving while dating back to the Middle Ages.

So, the real question becomes this: How long can I keep my company viable? And that is a very different matter. It comes down to several interrelated qualities:

- A healthy company culture
- A loyal workforce, reinforced by a reputation for fairness
- Internal advancement
- An environment of innovation and adaptability
- A larger purpose and goal (Lean But Not Mean)
- A viable succession program
- And most important: a potent and reliable decision-making process (the 5% Rule)

Companies grow old because they take these qualities for granted, growing complacent and assuming they will always be there rather than needing constant nurturing.

For example, after several generations of success, many companies begin offering unequal reward systems and promotions based on favoritism and tenure, not competence and productivity. Others decide they have grown so successful that nobody in the company can run it and go outside for talent. These changes can get further polarized as current generation of leaders retire and are replaced by a new crop of leaders, sometimes from outside the company and often with less tenure in the company.

Still others, influenced by company financial types or stock price, stop developing new products and coast on their aging "cash cow" catalog to maximize profits. And, of course, as we have noted throughout this book, some companies lose track of who they are and begin chasing opportunities without taking full consideration of what they are doing.

Finally, and this may be the quickest company killer of all: It fails at succession. How many great companies have all of us watched disintegrate because the current C-suite occupants refuse to let go, identifying themselves with the company and failing to realize that their time is past?

Or a board of directors that recruits a new CEO who uses the company to build their own reputation by utterly transforming the company into their own vision and destroying everything that once made the firm great.

Or the new chief executive who looks good on paper and says the right thing but ignores the company's established culture—its values and purpose—as out-of-date and irrelevant.

There are a lot of ways to ruin a great company over time. But there also are a few effective ways to keep them youthful even into old age. Every good company's duty is to last forever—for its customers, employees, and stakeholders—improving the business environment, rewarding those loyal to it, and making the world a better place. But to do that, they must survive and never forget what made them great. The goal of this section is to help you do that.

CHAPTER

15

Retention Is Its Own Engine

Preserve the Asset of Experience

We live in an era when keeping good employees is one of the biggest challenges faced by American business as well as many other regions of the world. Of course, employee retention has always been a concern, but in recent years it has become acute.

There is no shortage of "experts" proclaiming they have the answer. In 2018, it was the hot economy convincing workers to search elsewhere for better jobs. Then, during COVID it was the frustration of working at home. Then after the lockdown was lifted, it was the desire to find a job that still let employees continue to work at home. After that, it was inflation forcing workers to find new jobs to keep up with the rising cost of living.

175

There is always some external force beyond a company's control that can be blamed for its inability to hold on to employees—especially valuable, veteran employees.

But if that is the case, why do certain admired companies manage to keep their employees for decades, during good times and bad, without losing them? Why should employees leave during downturns when they have the least likely chance of finding a new—much less, better paying—job? And why should they leave during good times, abandoning everything from seniority to stock options, if they believe their current employer is taking care of them?

The truth is that employee retention is always an internal problem, not an external one. And I will go even further: If you are worrying about retaining your employees, then you already have a severe problem.

Why? Because your worry is a disguise for the fact that you already know that you may not be creating the best work environment for your people.

Companies that enjoy high employee morale do not worry about retention. They know they have it. If your employees are happy—and more important, feel empowered with control over their own lives—they aren't going anywhere. It is a win-win situation.

That is why I say that "retention is its own engine": if you are doing everything else right in terms of your employees, retention will take care of itself. If you need to announce that "we have to drive retention," you have already lost; you cannot explicitly drive retention. In fact, trying to do so will inevitably lead to making the situation worse.

Why?

Because you are solving one problem (supposedly) by creating another problem that may be even worse.

Here's what happens: By the time you realize that a valued employee is preparing to leave, it is essentially impossible to convince them to stay, short of buying them off or awarding them with a promotion—neither of which they likely have earned (if they do deserve either, then that's on you as a bad boss). But either way, the rest of your employees will have learned two things:

- First, that if you want more money and/or a bigger job in the company, then all you need to do is threaten to quit . . . and then blackmail the company to get your way.

- Second, that the company awards the most brazen con artists—not the employees who work the hardest or best or are the most loyal (indeed, just the opposite of the last). If you thought you had a problem with employee morale before, wait until you let a "departing" employee roll you.

Once again, and it has been a running theme in this book, is that a great company is always built on a philosophy of fairness, and that is especially true when it comes to keeping your people. Fairness may not retain that person who wishes to leave the company, but in dealing with them fairly (not retention bonus) you send a message to all your other employees. And that is why employee retention must be an outcome, not a goal.

If every day in every corner of your company, with every single action, you are not exhibiting trust in your employees, in convincing them that you are treating them fairly, then you will never be able to truly deal with the problem. Employees do not quit because circumstances have temporarily changed, they quit because they've long since decided that they will quit if they face one more setback or one more instance of being treated unfairly. And remember that disengaged employees have an outsized negative impact on the morale of those employees who want to stay. It is a matter of the quality of their working lives within the company—and you cannot improve that overnight. By the time they give you notice, they have already long-since checked out psychologically.

What do I mean by fairness? It is not so obvious as being nice to people, or even being objective in your decision-making. Those are understood. If you treat people differently because of who they are, as opposed to their intrinsic value, then you are a lost cause. But even if you do treat your employees properly, that is only the first step to the kind of fairness that makes them lifelong company loyalists—to the point that they remain loyal to your company even after circumstances have led them to move on.

Real fairness includes giving every employee that same opportunity to succeed. It also means making all eligible for a similar set of benefits. And it means recognizing that we all are flawed human beings who occasionally make mistakes or are biased in our judgments and, if we are penitent, deserve to be forgiven.

True fairness in business has two components: One is the perception of fairness—it is not enough to treat employees in a way you perceive as fair, but rather, in a way they feel is fair. And this is much harder to achieve because what you may believe is fair treatment based on several variables that cannot be shared with the employee (for example, giving a bigger raise to a coworker for superior work) can be judged by that employee as being deeply unfair. This is the great argument for transparency discussed in Chapter 4. You need to set the metrics in advance and reward accordingly. And if you are unable to do that, you must swallow hard and establish that every employee in that position should have an equal opportunity to get such a reward.

This goes so far against how most companies operate today that it may seem insane, but turning employees against each other because one party is jealous and angry over perceived unfairness is the perfect recipe for failed employee retention.

The second is personal liberty. Everyone wants control over their own life—and when they feel that life has become unfair, or unpredictable, or that their fate is in the hands of a quixotic or unreliable power that has no stake (or worse) in their personal happiness—they flee the circumstances in which they find themselves. And understandably so.

When employee departures rise to an unusual level, companies tend to blame the economy and the prospect of layoffs, and company observers suggest that the company itself may be in financial straits (or soon to enter them). But is that really the case? My sense is that beyond normal turnover due to employee life changes, unusual levels of employee departures are most often due either to the employer making those exiting employees feel as if they are boxed in by unfair rules and regulations or that the company is not treating them fairly by unequally awarding promotions, bonuses, and benefits, or both.

That is why the notion that some external cause is the reason that employees start streaming out of a company does not make sense on its face: Why would anyone quit a company that treats them fairly and lets them control their own destiny to go out into a failing economy with few job prospects? That is just an excuse for poor management.

Now, I should note that there is a third reason for employees—especially top-performing employees—leaving a company. It is the prospect of landing in a hot start-up enterprise that can offer a better job title and the prospect of founder stock options. This is especially the case—indeed, it is a way of life—in places like Silicon Valley.

My answer to that is to recognize that you are going to lose some of these people. It is inevitable: They are entrepreneurs, and entrepreneurs are destined to start their own enterprises and to pursue an extraordinary degree of freedom and have their own definition of control over their lives that no company but their own can offer them. And more power to them: People like that change the world for the better.

But the truth is that you do not really have to lose them for good. If you have great company built on fairness, in their hearts they will never leave you. Someday you may even buy their company or use their products to make your own company more successful. They may even, after a few years and a noble failure or two, come back to spend the remainder of their careers with you. But through it all, they will have fond memories of working with you, of your fairness. And precisely because you are fair, you will welcome them home with open arms.

As for your other top employees, the ones who are not so entrepreneurial, that fairness is the reason they will stay with you. If you provide them with new challenges, new responsibilities, and new opportunities on a regular basis, such that they feel they are being treated fairly, why should they leave for some other company for more money or a better title, but a loss of seniority and a worse work environment?

And that holds true for everyone in the company. How do you know that they are feeling properly and fairly treated, and are staying intellectually challenged with new challenges? By spending quality time with your employees in multiple settings. You cannot run a company by remote control and virtual meetings—you must get out of your office and regularly see your employees wherever they are. This is demanding work, consuming much of your daily life for years on end. But if you find yourself no longer up for the task, you should start looking for your replacement.

Prodigal Employees

Of course, for several reasons, there are employees who choose to leave for what they believe are greener pastures elsewhere. Our rule is that if they left NetScout on good terms and have not subsequently badmouthed the company, they will always be welcome back, if we have a suitable opening for them. Typically, they lose credit for their tenure with the company—but on several occasions, we have had employees who quit the company . . . and (in rare cases) even within a day or two, realized their mistake, and asked to return. We allowed them to do so without any penalties.

An interesting challenge to our philosophy of fairness is what to do with the acquisition of another company, which we do on a regular basis. Typically, when one company acquires another, especially a direct competitor, the employees of the acquired company could feel that they are second-class citizens—they are judged redundant and laid off, or they are demoted under their counterpart at the acquiring company, or they are forced to accept a reduced status of employee salary and benefits. Sometimes, there is a genuine overlap, such as two VPs of engineering.

Is this fair? Of course not. They were loyal to their old company, and they contributed to making that company worthy of our interest and acquisition. So, now are we to punish them for that? Fairness demands that every new employee, whether they were hired or transferred from an acquired company, deserves similar rights, benefits, and privileges as employees that have been with the company for years. And that, too, ideally, from the second they walk through the front door.

Now, there is one exception to this: the executive management of a "big-enough" acquired company. They are often redundant with our own executive staff; moreover, they have been the conveyors and enforcers of their own company's culture.

The history of the high-tech industry is filled with examples of companies that hired or acquired large groups of employees from a competitor—and ended up with an internal insurgency that nearly destroyed the company. As we have noted, this is one danger of offering earnouts to companies you are acquiring—and why we have a no-earn-out policy.

It is our philosophy that most new employees (who joined as part of the acquisition), because they are "true" NetScout employees, will find our culture so superior to the one where they came from that they will fully adopt the culture. And that has always proven to be the case. Those few people who refused to change usually leave quickly.

How does that jibe with the management of acquired companies? If they become employees, albeit briefly, of NetScout, how can they be let go and not violate NetScout's own fairness standards?

The answer is that part of the senior management team never become our employees: The fate of all executives of a company we are acquiring is settled during the acquisition negotiations. They know their fate—if they are being let go or (rarely) if asked to stay—long before the agreement is signed, and then they can make other plans. They also get a good severance package and typically have golden parachutes, and hence are generally not interested in staying, anyway. We never negotiate an acquisition without dealing with that factor—it is part of the 5% process. No company purchase is worth compromising our core philosophy.

That said, there are occasions that, as part of the deal, we allow some senior executives to stay on with NetScout for an interval of several months. That is largely so they can train our people on projects and processes for which NetScout has little prior experience. Moreover, if they prove to be a great fit for our culture, they may be asked if they would like to stay. But those scenarios are rare.

I should note that our definition of "senior management" does not go far down the organization chart. Everyone else in the acquired company is welcome and encouraged to join us, because part of the reasons for the acquisition is based on their talent and skill set.

They also may find themselves demoted slightly to report to a person who was once their equivalent (or vice versa), or they may see some salary adjustment to align it with their new NetScout peers (though the combination of salary and benefits we offer usually amounts to a de facto raise). But in our experience everyone from the acquired company stays and they quickly become happy and loyal employees—and are treated that way by company veterans. The process seems to work well. Today, more than 50% of NetScout executives are the former employees of an acquired company, and they have been with us on an average of 10+ years.

Is this a rational business strategy? It does not matter. It is fair and has delivered results for decades. Doesn't all this potential redundancy compromise the company? Not if we continue to innovate and grow, especially when we enjoy the synergistic effects of adding the products and customers of the acquired company.

Indeed, many of our new employees soon find themselves better off in terms of duties and salary than ever before. But what about during downturns—should you shed employees? Again, is that fair? If we have been following our Lean But Not Mean philosophy, we should already have been tightening our belts and not have to face the dire prospect of layoffs. Being vigilant in good times in preparation for tough times is also part of the 5% Rule. And if we do have to tighten even more, the sacrifice should be made by senior staff, rather than regular employees, because the former has a greater financial cushion.

Exceptional Times

Absorbing newly acquired companies while not compromising our core beliefs is not something we learned overnight. What has been most challenging is not compromising the notions of fairness and Lean But Not Mean in the main, but in the exceptional. Let me give you an example: With one of our corporate acquisitions, we found ourselves facing more than 100 new employees at an office in an overseas office, who expected that they would continue to receive a "retention bonus" that they were getting earlier in the acquired company. In other words, they wanted a bonus simply for allowing themselves to be integrated into NetScout.

Well, I waited a month to let them get a sense of our corporate culture, then I visited them. The first thing I told these new employees was, "There will not be any retention bonus" and they needed to get over the idea. Then, before they could complain I said to them, "But here's what I will do instead."

I put up a chart that contained five circles of assorted sizes. Then I explained that each of these circles represented a relative contribution to their new employees' compensation packages. As you might guess, the smallest of those circles was their actual salary. Larger circles included stock (which everybody got), annual bonuses (which everybody got), better benefits, and better job security (especially important, as this was a downtime in Silicon Valley), and biggest of all, quality of projects and quality of life—none of which were offered by the acquired company.

Last, I noted that everyone gets the same raises, the work cubicles are all the same size, that if they had a personal emergency they could leave the office without permission, and all the other features of Not Mean and Fairness.

After that nobody ever talked about leaving or retention bonuses. That was the moment that I understood retention as empowerment. The deciding factor for these new employees was not the salary or the retention bonus, but the chance to live out their dream of creating an important new product. To have enough control over that project to bring it to fruition with the blessing of their new employer.

Every one of those employees chose to stay with us. And the product we decided to source at that oversees location, as a proxy for "quality projects"? It became one of NetScout's most successful products. Would they have stayed with just a retention bonus? Perhaps, but not for long.

Life is about more than money. Indeed, when you are reduced to offering specific incentives to convince employees to stay, you have already lost. In choosing a temporary solution you have sacrificed the long game. In capturing the fake loyalty of a single employee, you have injected the distortions of jealousy and resentment into your entire employee ranks. You have shown everyone that when push comes to shove, you are willing to abandon any pretense of fairness—and that is a lesson your people will not soon forget. When the right moment comes, it will be their turn to blackmail you.

That is why I say that if you worry about employee retention, it is too late. That goal should have been implicit in every action you take as a leader. Establish a culture of fairness and never compromise that culture—even when it requires making tough decisions. Do that and you will never again worry about keeping your employees.

And believe me, that sure makes life a lot simpler and helps you to concentrate on other matters, like making the company an enduring success.

16

Golden Interns and Successful Succession

Retain Your Best for as Long as Possible

One of the biggest challenges that most companies face as they mature is also one they rarely address, except at the moment: How do you replace top employees, especially leaders, when they leave?

I do not know of a single company that has put in place a viable and scalable plan of succession—not just for the founder or CEO, though that looms huge in every enterprise—but also for top executives and managers, and even for the most talented and veteran employees.

The usual process is that a key employee announces their retirement, and then there is a scramble to put out a job opening listing or hire a recruiter. Then when a list of candidates is developed, weeks or months of interviews take place—all under the gun of the critical employee's pending departure.

Then, as the list is being whittled down to a couple candidates, the current holder of that office is physically and psychologically checking out and going through the usual round of good-byes and a retirement party or two.

Finally, on a pre-appointed day, the retiring employee is gone. The replacement arrives at the office, ready to take over the job—but only after a learning curve of a few months.

Think about that. Consider what is being lost. The departing employee, who is sometimes never seen again, takes with them years, even decades, of experience. That person knows as well as anyone just how the company works, what mistakes were made in the past, and how to negotiate the company bureaucracy to get things. They may have developed deep and enduring relationships with key employees and have been a fount of wisdom for younger employees. They are the company's institutional memory.

Now without conveying all that knowledge and experience to their replacement—much less to everyone else in the company—they have disappeared from the face of the earth. What an enormous loss of intellectual capital for the company! And yet, most companies accept this as a matter of course.

Meanwhile, the replacement, no matter how capable and competent, is still going to take months or years to learn what has just been so casually lost. And even if this new employee does, in time, become just as valuable—there is the prospect, not that far off, when they, too, will disappear.

Companies obsess about cutting waste in overhead, bonuses, operating costs, and new ventures—yet how many millions of dollars do they lose every time a key employee walks out the door with their gold watch? And how much more devastating is it when the CEO, or worse, the founder, leaves.

I have seen one great corporation after another start the downhill path to oblivion the day the person who built the company leaves; in fact, I worked for one such company many decades ago, before cofounding NetScout. For every Tim Cook at Apple, there have been dozens of other firms that did not survive succession at the top. If you want to know what obsesses company founders and long-time CEOs, it is precisely that.

The question of succession and the loss of intellectual capital has haunted me for many years—and it has become increasingly acute now that I can see that day in my own future. Why have companies always treated this process as inevitable?

A few years ago, as is my way, I decided to take a different path. I am still implementing it, so I cannot quote you a pile of evidence in its support, but by early measure this model seems to be succeeding. Let me share with you how it works.

At NetScout, succession is not overnight, but instead a multiyear program, with time span directly proportional to level and importance of the corresponding senior or executive leader. That is enough time for the departing and arriving individuals to interact closely and for experience to be shared. It also removes much of the politicking that characterizes much of office life, in which the ambitious maneuver to displace their superior.

Take, for example, a member of the company's C-suite (for example, CFO or even CRO). This CXO, after 20 years with the company, is not only reaching retirement age but also is well-off enough to even retire a few months early. The CEO is aware of this and asks the CXO, when they are ready, to set a firm date for their departure.

The CEO now puts into place the three-phase succession program.

In phase one, the CEO, working with the current CXO, identifies the candidate in the company to become the new CXO. Let us say that there are two or three people reporting to the current CXO (or an outside candidate in rare cases). After watching them in action for several months, and in consultation with the current CXO, the CEO designates the CXO-designate, or Acting CXO, of the three.

This will have obvious consequences. One or both other two candidates may consider leaving the company. But instead of creating bad blood at the last moment, this process can be done smoothly and quietly, with an extended chance for these solid employees to still decide to stay with the company.

Meanwhile, the chosen candidate can begin the process, without actual responsibility, of learning the CXO's job.

In phase two, the succession is made official, but only inside the company. The successor now wears the title of "Acting CXO."

During this phase, the acting CXO begins to take on, under the CXO's tutelage, one after another of various jobs of the CXO inside the company. To the outside world—customers, investors, board of directors, and so forth, nothing has changed—the current CXO still holds the position and title, and the future CXO is a secondary and disconnected figure other than for a few preliminary introductions. The current CXO remains the face of the company's financial operations to the outside world.

This second phase is the vital one and will require a certain amount of patience from everyone involved. The task of the successor is to learn everything possible about the new job, and to bring into the process their own experience with the company. (NetScout only promotes from within.)

For the current CXO, the challenge is to use that year to convey as much wisdom as they can, to accept the inevitability of mistakes and use them to teach their successor a better solution, and to systematically surrender pieces of responsibility to the replacement.

Finally, at the beginning of phase three the ascension of the acting CXO to the title of CXO is officially announced. At this point, it will be old news to employees of the company, but fresh to the outside world. The old CXO will step down and the new CXO will assume all the duties of their predecessor.

But now instead of being dropped into a position where they know only a fraction of what is needed for success, the new CXO will be arriving at that position after more than one year of on-the-job training. If this process is done properly, the company's operations should not miss a beat.

And what of the retiring CXO? This may be the most innovative part of this succession. They do not just disappear into the night. This person, now "CXO emeritus" is expected to stay with the company one more year in a mentoring/advisory role to the new CXO.

What this means is that the CXO emeritus is given enough time, while preparing for full retirement, in which they are to be available when needed by the new CXO for advice, contacts and introductions, and consultation when needed. They are not required to come into the office or attend meetings, unless asked—just to be on call.

In exchange, the CXO emeritus is well compensated and has all the employees' health benefits, and they can continue to vest any unvested shares. They also cannot consult any company competitors during that interval—which is a benefit for the company. And they are treated with full honors for their distinguished service.

The emeritus position can prove to be a nice transition into retirement—not the usual, shocking jump that leaves many retirees lost and bitter.

Smart executives will make effective use of their emeritus predecessors. By now they will know them well—and just as important, they will not feel as threatened as they would be going to their peers for advice.

Company-Wide Succession

Once you get a sense of the power of the three-stage succession model it suddenly becomes apparent that it can be implemented among all your company senior and important alumni.

We are currently amid putting into place at NetScout what I am calling the Golden Intern program. The title is a bit tongue-in-cheek, because when we hear the word *intern* we usually envisage an ardent college student working summer break at a law firm or a corporate office in hopes of getting work experience and, with luck, a nice recommendation letter.

In fact, our "interns" are more likely to be senior citizens who already have had brilliant careers and enjoy enormous respect from the people they assist.

Some of you may remember the 2015 Hollywood movie *The Intern*. This is one of my favorite movies because of its creative script and acting, and because I could identify myself in both the Anne Hathaway budding entrepreneur character, and the Robert De Niro recently retired character. As a lifelong entrepreneur contemplating my own retirement and succession plans, the plights of both characters resonated with me. The name and some of the ideas in this chapter are in fact inspired by *The Intern*. Separately, NetScout is also in the process of exploring the creation of a "NETSCOUT Alumni Network." The idea may seem radical, but it is anything but new. Many mature companies have alumni organizations, some with chapters around the country. Many are informal: a way for former employees to get together socially and reminisce about their time at the company, as well (if they are still working) to network about job opportunities.

Some companies take the next step and imbue their alumni groups with additional power and influence. These companies sometimes hold alumni gatherings at their facilities, bring in executives as guest speakers, and use them to pre-introduce new products.

With our Golden Interns program, we are taking the traditional alumni model even further. If you are dedicated to fairness in your company, of sharing with them ownership, and of trusting them to implementing the other 95% of your 5% decisions, why should you be surprised when they retain a deep emotional connection and loyalty to the company even after they depart? Who knows more—and cares more—about NetScout than those individuals who dedicated their careers to the company? And who better to notice when we are repeating the mistakes, and successes, of the past?

Given the depth of institutional knowledge they have gained after carrying that decision-making responsibility for years, why not want to stay connected with that wisdom?

Let me give you another example, this one from my own life. I've now reached the age when many of the physicians I have gone to all my life have now retired. It is a common experience we all eventually face that a wise older doctor you have always depended on, who may even have become a friend, enters old age before you do.

Now, your new doctor is also much younger than you—some even look to you like kids. They have all the right credentials, and they seem very good at what they do, but you have doubts. Where do you go for your second opinion?

Not to another young doctor. Ideally, you have maintained contact with your old doctor, the one who knows everything about your health history, your past illnesses, and your various drug reactions. If they are still available to you for anything from a quick phone call to a private consultation, wouldn't you take advantage of that resource? Wouldn't you feel much more comfortable if that veteran doctor's opinion validated the younger doctor's judgment?

It is important to note that Golden Interns are not strictly company alumni. They are two different programs. Alumni groups are a mechanism for former colleagues to keep in touch with one another, learn about what the company is doing, and be a resource to the company in the sense of creating a body of loyal—and, when needed—vocal supporters and shareholders.

Golden Interns are much more engaged with the company. This is underscored by the fact that one cannot simply sign up to be a Golden Intern. Rather, they need to be invited—and that invitation is a function of their current life status and how they can materially contribute to the success of the company. It is not a sentimental title—that venerable retired ex-VP may not be invited as their skills are no longer applicable, and that lower-level employee who was an expert at running the travel office or IT troubleshooting might get an immediate invitation to become a Golden Intern on the day they retire.

What do Golden Interns do? They act as sounding boards, they mentor, they consult. Interestingly, we have found that one of the most important things they offer is trust. C-level executives understandably are wary about going to the most obvious sources, the CEO and the board of directors, for advice, be it personal, or about their career, or about an important business decision. But a Golden Intern, who has held that employee's title, represents no threat and no competition, and thus can give honest feedback to a business scenario.

Recent studies have shown that many high-powered people still are working and contributing into their 80s. What that means is that these "retired" people are immensely valuable—and at a time in their lives when they may be looking for a new purpose, being a Golden Intern may be an immensely rewarding choice—not least because they can do it from anywhere in the world.

The official duration of being a Golden Intern is one year, though those interns who prove particularly valuable as a mentor or advisor, or who make a measurable contribution to the firm's continued success, may be asked to stay on another year—and then re-upped on an annual basis as long as both they and the company remain interested.

The sheer value of these Golden Interns in terms of maintaining continuity in the company (a crucial factor as the company matures) and as guardians of the company's history and core philosophy is almost incalculable. Companies, as they grow older, often drift off-course as new blood operates without any understanding of company precedent. Having true veterans on hand to act as course correctors is a vital stabilizer that no handbook of company policy can ever duplicate.

The three-phase succession program and the Golden Intern programs are just being launched at NetScout, but the early results are promising—and comforting in the knowledge that who we are will not be lost in the years ahead.

In the meantime, I am working on the challenge of succession for a cofounder and CEO. That day is looming ahead—and has begun to capture much more of my 5%.

What will be my solution? Stay tuned in the months and years ahead.

CHAPTER
17

Fair, Fast, and Built to Last

The Keys to a Great and Enduring Company

At the beginning of this book, I wrote about the 5% Rule as it applied to acquisitions. But, over the years, as the subsequent chapters have shown, I realize that this same rule can be applied throughout an organization, not just across departments, but also up and down the organization chart.

In fact, as time passes, I am more convinced than ever that it is almost impossible to become an enduring Lean But Not Mean company without the widespread implementation of the 5% Rule in every major decision or strategy the enterprise undertakes.

I did not always believe this. In fact, for the first couple of decades running NetScout, I had never even thought of the 5% Rule. I did business like any other CEO. That is, I got involved in negotiations and initiatives as needed, sometimes stepping in at the beginning, other times not getting involved until they were well along, and sometimes just showing up to sign the final agreement.

But as time went on, I noticed that one of the commonalities of successful company projects was the fact that I had been involved early, before the process was too far along and the commitments were too deep. I also noticed that when I got involved later—or for that matter, stayed involved too long—that these initiatives had much less chance of success, cost more, and took much longer to complete.

I have already told the story of one of our operations in Europe and how we had to shut it down. I used it as an example of how to handle such an event humanely. But that was only part of the story. The other part is that the reason we got into such an unpleasant situation to begin with is because I did not become sufficiently involved at the start. We never should have made that acquisition in the first place! But we were too distracted at that time to see that. By the time I did get involved, the acquisition had taken on a life of its own, and as a result, I let it go on. So, it is nice to pat myself on the back for handling the shutdown so humanely, but I also must take the blame for letting that situation deteriorate in the first place.

That experience led me to rethink my role in the acquisition process. Why had some acquisitions worked so well, and others hadn't, and what was my contribution to each?

That led to my epiphany: We had the greatest chance of success when I got involved in the decision-making at the very start—in the first 5% of the process—established the strategy and direction of the deal, then got out of the way of the team responsible of executing the project.

I have been using this 5% Rule explicitly for more than a decade, implicitly for two decades, and accidentally before that. It turned out that using the 5% Rule in acquisitions saves time and money, it spares your talented team members from wasting their time, and it insulates everybody from the nightmare of getting involved in a failed project that has too much momentum to stop.

That was just the start. Since then, I have discovered that the 5% Rule can work as a powerful management tool for the entire company. The 5% Rule operates on both the horizontal (across functional operations) and vertical (down the organizational chart) axes of a company's business.

The first time you implement the 5% Rule it is likely to be awkward, but in time you will get smooth at it—its processes and procedures will soon be well established, your staff will become accustomed to you being deeply involved at the starts and then stepping away. It will get even easier when you realize that the final 5% for a given project is often the kick-off for the initial 5% of the next project.

5% Throughout the Organization

Perhaps not surprisingly, NetScout's employees are perfectly happy to let me execute the 5% Rule: It takes some of the responsibility for decision-making off them.

But they are learning that when I say the 5% Rule is universal, they need to implement it in their own work as well, especially at the leadership levels—leaders are the "conductors of orchestra." It will take time and a lot of educating, but I remain indomitable: A company can never truly rise to its full potential unless it operates top to bottom, side to side, under the influence of the 5% Rule.

When that day comes—and we are well on our way at NetScout—my 5% Rule decisions will immediately initiate 5% Rule decisions by the people who report to me, then a similar set of decisions by those who report to them, and so on, until one day, when one of my managers asks me, "When are you having your 5% meeting?" I am going to reply, "When are you having yours?"

An (Unexpectedly) Universal Rule

The 5% Rule also holds in compensation. Though we do not disclose salaries and rewards between employees, I do establish, up front, the rules for compensation throughout the company. My personal rule is that, on some rare occasions that compensation information is leaked accidentally, we have a logical rationale for every decision.

In my experience, the 5% Rule also holds true for branding, messaging, positioning, going into new markets, opening new facilities, sales targets, stock plans, and so on, through every part of the company.

Take product development, for example. My 5% participation rarely has to do with details of the proposed product, performance specs, pricing, or any of the usual stuff associated with a senior executive. Rather, my usual role is to ask one specific question, "Why are we offering this product?" If I do not get a well-considered answer, I can only assume that the product is being pursued because it seems like the right thing to do, and that is not an adequate answer. If we cannot explain a new product to ourselves, how can we explain it to prospective customers?

The 5% Rule also helps to explain other practices described in this book. As another example, consider the process I have described as being willing to "leave money on the table."

At its heart, it is simply another application of the 5% Rule: If I have already determined at the start what constitutes success, then I have the metric in hand for deciding when I see it, and the process is done. There is no need to go on.

Trust and The 5% Rule

This brings us to the second axis: the organization chart. If the 5% Rule can be applied successfully to every department in the company, why can't it also be applied at every level of the company?

Sure, the 5% Rule is a critical—even the critical—part of my job as CEO. But why should it not be an important part of the job of every executive, manager, and supervisor in the company? They too are leading teams that are taking on projects and initiatives; those teams also deserve to not waste their time and energy. They too deserve 5% leadership, from leaders who establish the path and goals at the start, then let the teams do their jobs.

There is, in fact, a famous precedent for this philosophy from many years ago. Once again, we look to Hewlett-Packard (HP), that benchmark of enlightened management under its two founders. HP instituted a rule that decision-making should always be pushed down through the organization to the individual closest to the problem, even if that individual was at the lowest level of the company.

Where HP, in the past, were trying to solve the problem of decision-making with limited information, today the challenge is decision-making with limited time. The internet, big data, broadband communications, and now AI have changed everything.

These days we are not short of information. On the contrary, we are inundated with it. Now we are short on time—hence a rush to execute an initiative, before spending quality time on the kind of decision-making that could drive superior execution. As business time continues to accelerate, windows of opportunity grow ever shorter.

Now the decisions we used to make over the course of weeks sometimes need to be made in minutes. Too often, all that you have time to do is make some quick choices, set the rules for the road ahead, and then move on to the next decision to be made. Hence, the 5% Rule.

But you may ask, if events in the business world are occurring at an unprecedented rate—and thus, decisions must be made in shorter time than ever—how can the 5% Rule, with its careful deliberation before every decision, work?

Let me suggest two reasons why the 5% Rule is better suited to our chaotic times than any comparable strategy. The first is to compare the overall time expected. Yes, the go/no go process under the 5% Rule is much slower than leaping onto a new opportunity the moment it presents itself. But once that decision is made under the 5% Rule, the resources of the entire company are aligned and directed at its execution, and its participants trusted to make their own decisions on clearly defined goals.

For example, in software engineering: Which is faster, cutting the actual lines of code to write, based on the 5% Rule and thinking ahead, versus rushing to write the longest program in the shortest time?

In other words, compared to the inevitable chaos of goals, responsibilities, approvals, and resource distribution experienced by a company that chases an opportunity before it even knows how to do it, a 5% Rule company, in the end, is going to be quicker in its full response.

The second reason is the likelihood of success. The 5% Rule company begins having very specific and realizable goals; it is also less likely to be diverted or distracted from its chosen path, it is less likely to head down dead ends and lose time and money, and, most important, less likely to treat its employees unfairly by cancelling the project and laying off loyal people (and taking write-downs that punish shareholders).

Just ask yourself: How often have you seen excited companies leap onto the next big thing—and end up cancelling that venture a few months later?

A company built on trust and implementing the 5% Rule everywhere has the greatest chance of success and a long life.

Epilogue

I conclude this narrative with a thought experiment.

What if were to build a great company that had a reputation for innovation, fairness and equity, continuous growth, high employee morale and customer loyalty, and had the potential to last for generations? What would such a company look like?

We have seen a few examples of such enterprises over recent history. Would you characterize any of them as rapidly chasing every next big thing? Would they be known for endless layoffs to boost their bottom line? Would they suffer lousy employee morale, or for overcharging their customers, or for treating their acquisitions like second-class company citizens? And how many would be notorious for not considering their actions before making them?

You can name a few current high-flying companies that have some or all these characteristics. Would you work for one of them? Would you run one of them? Most of all, would you bet everything on them surviving over the long term?

In the end, all of us want in our careers to be treated fairly, not to deal with different rules for different people or working hard for a management that fires us for their own mistakes. And we want to work for a company that rewards and advances us for our hard work and loyalty, that gives us a chance to stay as long as we want to—and keeps us in the family even after we leave. And we want to work for a company for which we are proud.

Look around you: How many companies today are like that? How many companies could even be like that, even if they wanted to? Now ask yourself, why then stick to business practices and uphold corporate cultures that do not work? Why not try something new?

The 5% Rule could be that "something new." It is a new way of looking at business organization and management that is both novel and yet still captures the spirit of the old and proven way of working. Best of all, I know it works.

We all want to be part of an organization that has the competitive efficiency (the Leanness) to make it a success, but also the fairness (the Not Mean) to make it a happy place to work. But no company can ever achieve the goal of becoming Lean But Not Mean operating under the current status quo of business life.

It needs the added tool of the 5% Rule.

Care to join me?

Run your company as if you want it to live forever.

Index

Notes

Notes